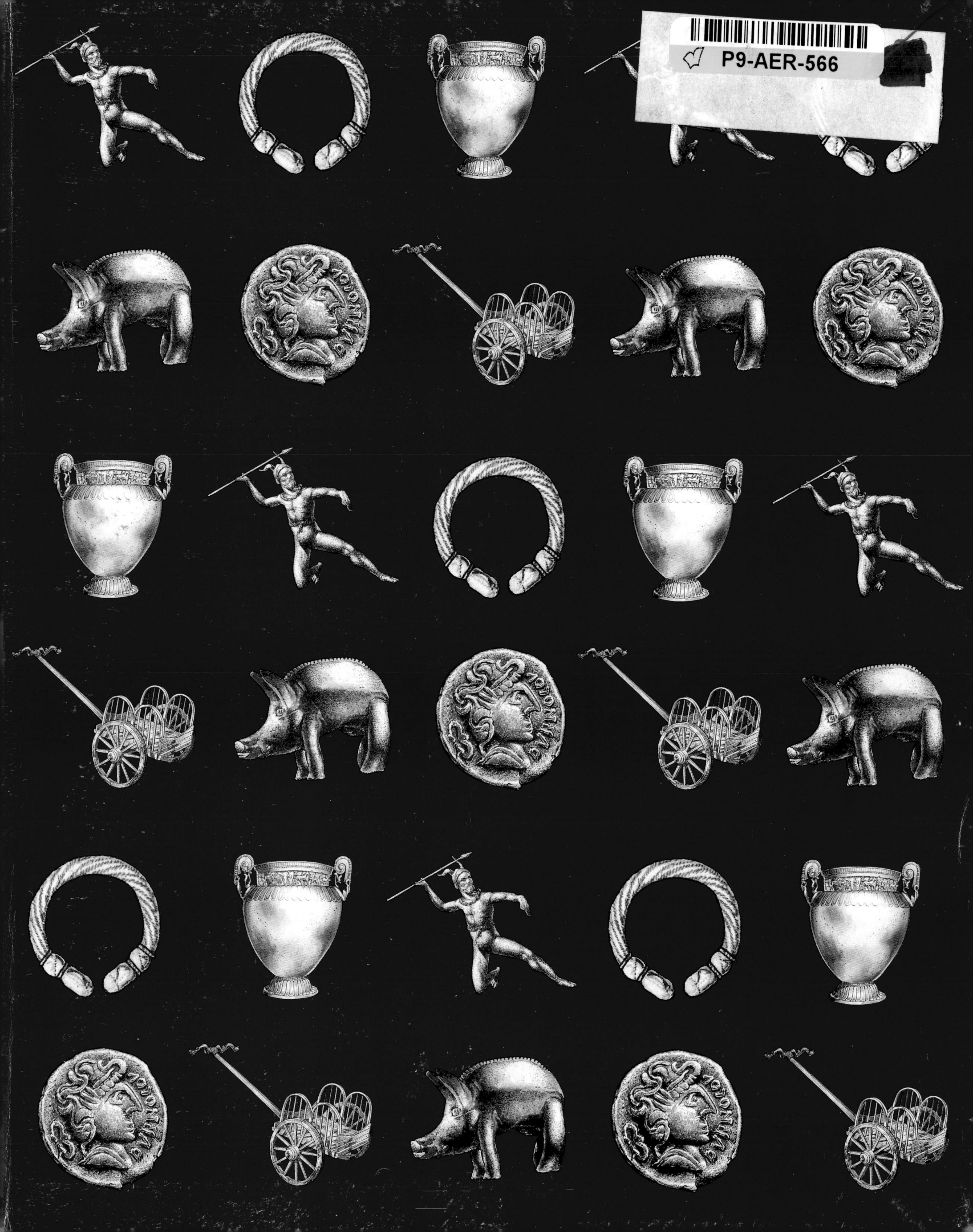
P9-AER-566

THE CELTS

HAZEL MARY MARTELL

Acknowledgments

The publishers would like to thank Mrs. M. Fry at Historic Scotland, and Nick Brannon and Anne Hamlin at the Department of the Environment for Northern Ireland, for their assistance in the preparation of this book; Bill Le Fever, who illustrated the see-through pages; and the organizations that have given their permission to reproduce the following pictures:

Archiv für Kunst und Geschichte/Eric Lessing: 4-5, 5 top, 9 center bottom, 12-13.
Ancient Art and Architecture Collection: 24 top, 27 bottom right, 34 top, 45 top right, /Ronald Sheridan 10 top, 11 top, 13 bottom, /Brian Wilson 9 top right.
Bibliothèque Nationale: 34 bottom, 38 top left. **Bridgeman Art Library/British Museum:** 20 top left.
British Museum: 15 top, 18 top left. **C.M. Dixon/Photo Resources:** 23 top right.
Explorer/A. Le Toquin: 27 center right. **Historisches Museum Basel/M. Babey:** 29 bottom right.
Historic Scotland: 32. **Simon James:** 23 bottom left. **Life File/Tony Abbott:** 14 top.
The Menil Collection /Hickey-Robertson: 27 center left.
Moravske Zemske Muzeum: 27 bottom center. **Musée d'art et d'histoire, Geneva:** 31 bottom right.
Museum Carolino Augusteum, Salzburg: 12 top. **National Museum of Ireland:** 21 center.
National Museums of Scotland: 45 bottom right. **National Museum of Wales:** 28 top left.
Photographie Giraudon/Chatilloon-sur-Seine, Mus. Archeologique: 21 bottom right, /Musée des Antiquites Nationales, Saint Germain en Laye 9 center top, /Rueil-Malmaison, Mus. Nat. de Château de Malmaison 43 top right.
RCS Libri & Grandi Opere Spa/Muzeul National de Istorie a Romaneiei: 37 top left.
Réunion des Musées Nationaux/Musée des Antiquites Nationales: 19 top right, 27 top.
Scala/Rheinisches Landesmuseum, Bonn: 7 bottom, /Museo del Terme, Rome 39 right.
Society of Antiquaries of London/Geremy Butler: 5 bottom right.
Ville de Beaune, Conservation des Musées/Musée du Vin de Bourgogne/M. Couval: 23 top left.
Werner Forman Archive/British Museum: 8 bottom right, 9 top left, 13 top right, 35 bottom, 37 top right, /National Museum of Ireland 31 top right, /National Museum of Wales 27 bottom left.
Württembergisches Landesmuseum: 25 top.

Illustrators
Richard Berridge: 28, 29, 30-31, 36, 37.
Peter Bull: 7, 29, 38.
James Field: cover, 42, 44, 45, 46-47.
Ray Grinaway: 8, 9, 10, 11, 20, 21, 43.
Bill Le Fever: heading icons, 16-17, 24-25, 32-33, 40-41.
Tony Randall: 12, 13, 14, 15.
Mark Stacey: 4, 6, 18, 19, 34, 35.
Simon Williams: 22, 23, 26, 38-39.

Published by the Penguin Group
Penguin USA, 375 Hudson Street, New York, New York 10014, U.S.A.
Penguin Books Ltd, 27 Wrights Lane, London W8 5TZ, England
Penguin Books Australia Ltd, Ringwood, Victoria, Australia
Penguin Books Canada Ltd, 10 Alcorn Avenue, Toronto, Ontario, Canada M4V 3B2
Penguin Books (N.Z.) Ltd, 182–190 Wairau Road, Auckland 10, New Zealand

Penguin Books Ltd, Registered Offices: Harmondsworth, Middlesex, England

First published in Great Britain by Hamlyn Children's Books, an imprint of Reed Children's Books Limited, 1994
First published in the United States of America by Viking, a division of Penguin Books USA Inc., 1996

1 3 5 7 9 10 8 6 4 2

Library of Congress Catalog Card Number: 95–61265

ISBN 0–670–86558–3

Printed in Belgium

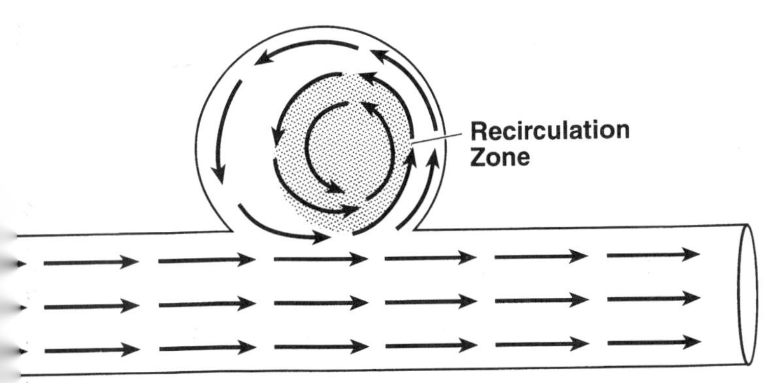

. Schematic diagram showing the hemodynamic circulation patterns
eurysm.

erted to turbulence.[130] Blood flow proceeds from the parent ves-
aneurysm at the distal or downstream extent of the aneurysm
ates around the periphery along the aneurysm wall from the
top of the fundus (downstream to upstream), returning in a type
shower" along the aneurysm wall toward the neck region, and
oximal or closest extent of the aneurysm neck into the parent
6.11).[131] As flow persists, areas of stagnation or vortices devel-
central zone of the aneurysm. These rotating vortices, formed
nce to the aneurysm at each systole and then circulated around
n, are caused by the slipstreams or regions of recirculating flow
themselves when entering the aneurysm at its downstream wall
le.[132] The stagnant vortex zone occurs in the center and at the
oper portion of the aneurysm and becomes more pronounced in
ysms. These hemodynamic patterns are depicted in Fig. 6.12. It
nt zone that is believed to promote the formation of thrombi or
particularly in giant aneurysms.

pture of Saccular Aneurysms

ntracranial aneurysms occurs in 28 000 North Americans each
proximately 50% of these people dying within the first 30 days
pture.[133] The rupture of a cerebral aneurysm occurs when the
e aneurysm wall exceeds the force produced by the structural
When an intracranial saccular aneurysm ruptures, blood is
a pressure of approximately 100 mm Hg into the subarachnoid
a pressure of 0 to 10 mm Hg is prevalent under normal cir-
[34] The aneurysm wall, fully distended prior to rupture, consists
collagen, which bears the majority of the mechanical response
ress induced by the tension. The strength of the aneurysm wall

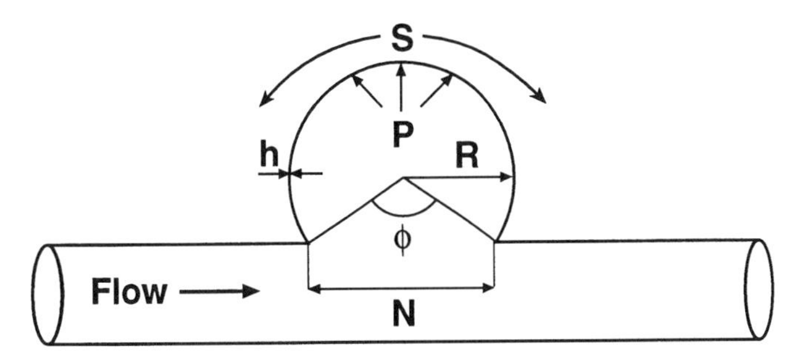

FIGURE 6.10. A cross-sectional view of the saccular aneurysm employed in the biomathematical model. P represents intra-aneurysmal pressure; S, circumferential stress; R, aneurysm radius; N, neck diameter; h, wall thickness; ϕ, neck angle (angle of wall closure).

diameter N ranges in size from 1.5 to 10.0 mm and is classified as small ($N \leq 4.0$ mm) or wide ($N > 4.0$ mm) with an average neck diameter $N = 4.0$ mm.[127] The variables ϕ and N are related by the following relation[70]:

$$\frac{N}{2} = R \sin \frac{\phi}{2}. \tag{6.26}$$

Defining the parameter ξ, which is dependent on time, as the displacement at some later time from R to $R + \xi(t)$, the strain ε of the expanded aneurysm is then given by[128]

$$\varepsilon = \frac{S}{E} = \frac{\xi A}{\Sigma R}, \tag{6.27}$$

where A is the area of the aneurysm neck, Σ is the surface area of the aneurysm fundus or dome, and R is the original aneurysm radius. S can also be expressed, according to Laplace's law for a spherical elastic object, as

$$S = \frac{PR}{2h}, \tag{6.16}$$

where P is the intra-aneurysmal pressure.

An equation of motion describing the vibrational displacement of the aneurysm wall can be derived by considering the forces acting on the aneurysm in static equilibrium. These include forces due to pressure ($\mathbf{F}_{\text{pres}}$), circumferential stress ($\mathbf{F}_{\text{stress}}$), and inertia ($\mathbf{F}_{\text{iner}}$). $\mathbf{F}_{\text{pres}}$ is a distending or pushing force that acts in an outward direction while the other forces, i.e., $\mathbf{F}_{\text{iner}}$ and $\mathbf{F}_{\text{stress}}$, are compressive forces and act in a direction opposite to $\mathbf{F}_{\text{pres}}$. The balance of forces written in equation form are

$$\mathbf{F}_{\text{pres}} = \mathbf{F}_{\text{stress}} + \mathbf{F}_{\text{iner}}. \tag{6.28}$$

Since the motion of the aneurysm is driven by a pulsatile pressure function, a more accurate characterization of the dynamics of the aneurysm can be obtained by expressing Eq. (6.28) as the balance of pressures (force per unit surface area within the aneurysm) instead of forces:

$$\mathbf{P} = \mathbf{P}_{\text{stress}} + \mathbf{P}_{\text{iner}}. \tag{6.29}$$

P represents the pulsatile driving force exerted on the aneurysm wall, which is related directly to the intra-aneurysmal pressure.

$\mathbf{P}_{\text{stress}}$ is the pressure or force exerted on the aneurysm wall by the circumferential stress and can be determined by setting Eq. (6.27) equal to Eq. (6.15) and solving for P:

$$\frac{PR}{2h} = E\,\frac{\xi A}{\Sigma R}, \tag{6.30}$$

$$\mathbf{P}_{\text{stress}} = 2hE\,\frac{\xi A}{\Sigma R^2}. \tag{6.31}$$

Equation (6.31) can be further simplified by

$$\mathbf{P}_{\text{stress}} = B\xi, \tag{6.32}$$

where $B = 2hEA/(\Sigma R^2)$.

$\mathbf{F}_{\text{iner}}$ is the inertial force due to the acceleration of the aneurysm wall and is equal to, according to Newton's second law,

$$\mathbf{F}_{\text{iner}} = ma \tag{6.33}$$

where m is the object mass and a is the acceleration of the object. Since the intracranial aneurysm is blood-filled, the inertial force term consists of the mass of the blood in the aneurysm and mass of the aneurysm wall and is represented by the system's kinetic energy, which is concentrated in the vicinity of the aneurysm neck,[128]

$$\mathbf{F}_{\text{iner}} = m_b a = \frac{1}{2} m_b \frac{d^2\xi}{dt^2}, \tag{6.34}$$

where m_b, the mass of blood, can be approximated by

$$m_b \approx 0.8\rho_b a A \tag{6.35}$$

where ρ_b is the density of blood, a is the aneurysm neck radius, and A is the aneurysm neck area. Also from Eq. (6.34), $d^2\xi/dt^2$ is the acceleration of the blood-filled aneurysm wall in response to an external driving force. The pressure due to inertia, $\mathbf{P}_{\text{iner}}$, is

$$\mathbf{P}_{\text{iner}} = \frac{\mathbf{F}_{\text{iner}}}{A} = \frac{1}{2}(0.8\rho_b a)\frac{d^2\xi}{dt^2}. \tag{6.36}$$

Similar to the other components of pressure, $\mathbf{P}_{\text{iner}}$ can be simplified accord-

ing to

$$\mathbf{P}_{\text{iner}} = A$$

where $A = \frac{1}{2}(0.8\rho_b a)$.

Substituting the components of pressu
into Eq. (6.29) yields the following differ

$$P = \frac{1}{2}(0.8\rho_b a)\frac{d^2}{dt}$$

Equation (6.38), which is a linear, no
ential equation, can be rewritten as

$$P = A\,\frac{d^2\xi}{dt^2}$$

The pressure P can be represented as th
flow and is stated mathematically as

$$P = F_{\text{bp}}\ \text{cc}$$

where F_{bp} is the pulsatile hemodynamic
pressure and ω_{df} is the frequency of
then rewritten as

$$A\,\frac{d^2\xi}{dt^2} + B\xi =$$

Equation (6.41) demonstrates that it i
cally the vibrational properties of the
given later in the chapter, yields the sp
response to a driving force with resp
can be used to determine the resonan
investigate the effects of external force
a physical basis for the influence of re
also be discussed later in the chapter.

6.4.2.2 Intra-Aneurysmal Hemodyn

Up to this point, the description of
been limited to the statics and dyna
intra-aneurysmal hemodynamics. Blo
regular and predictable according pr
between the aneurysm and its paren
parent artery with an aneurysm, div
the inlet of the aneurysm, leads to
effect producing increased lateral pr

FIGURE 6.1
within an a

easily conv
sel into the
neck, circu
neck to the
of "isotrop
exits the p
vessel (Fig
ops within
at the entr
the aneurys
rolling upo
during syst
fundus or u
larger aneu
is this stagn
blood clots,

6.4.3 R

Rupture of
year with a
following ru
tension of t
components
forced unde
space, wher
cumstances.
primarily of
against the

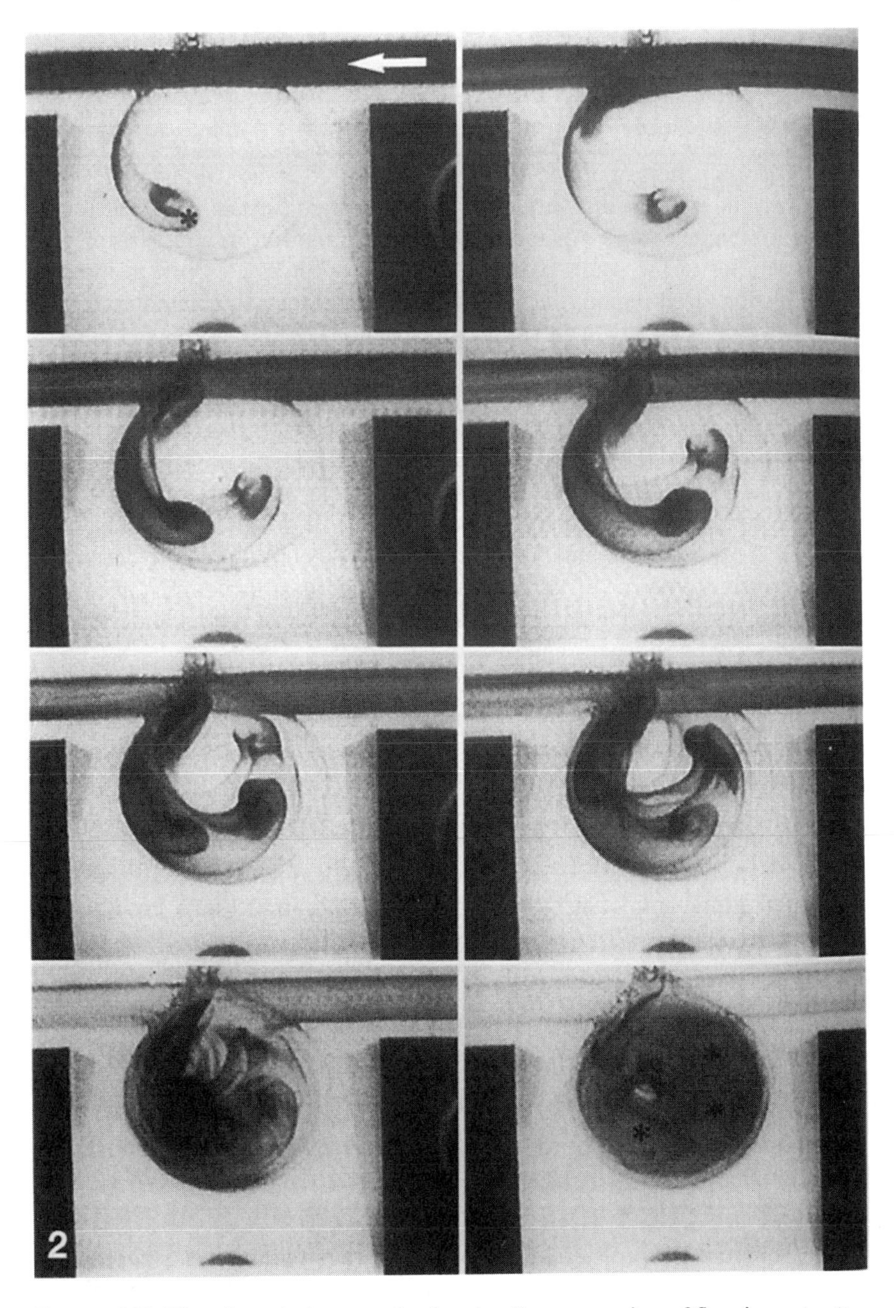

FIGURE 6.12. Time-lapsed photographs showing the progression of flow in an *in vitro* aneurysm phantom using (1) steady flow and (2) pulsatile flow. (Reprinted, with permission, from *Neuroradiology*, **36**, 530–536. Y.P. Gobin, J.L. Counord, P. Flaud, and J. Duffaux, In vitro study of hemodynamics in a giant saccular aneurysm model: Influence of flow dynamics in the parent vessel and effects of coil embolization. © 1994 Springer-Verlag Berlin.)

will only be as strong as its weakest point. Thus, the previously mentioned force required to induce rupture is directly related to the force needed to exceed the "breaking point" or elastic limit of collagen defined quantitatively by the elastic or Young's modulus. The terms *elastic modulus* and *Young's modulus* imply the same measurement and are often used interchangeably. However, the inner wall is not isotropic, i.e., there exists a localized region that is in a much more advanced state of degradation in comparison with the remainder of the wall. As the hemodynamic forces continue to impinge upon this localized region, the aneurysm wall continues to expand uniformly with the underlying collagen within this localized region in a higher state of stress.[135] In response to the large magnitude of stress, the aneurysm wall "breaks," resulting in a slight crack. In applications that can be drawn from the engineering sciences, a pressurized elastic sphere with a crack exhibits a much higher increase in tension around the immediate area of the crack. The location and dimensions of the crack depend primarily on the surface energy per unit area, which is a property unique to the aneurysm tissue, i.e., collagen. This is compounded by the load of the external pressure developed by the constant volume of tethered tissue acting on or against the aneurysm wall. These two factors acting in concert are sufficient to precipitate rupture at the localized weakened region.

In addition to the processes involved in the development of aneurysms, intra-aneurysmal hemodynamics are also important in the rupture of aneurysms. Figure 6.13 depicts the intra-aneurysmal hemodynamic patterns in a ruptured aneurysm from a theoretical and experimental standpoint. Once an aneurysm ruptures or bleeds, blood seeps into the subarachnoid space of adjacent brain tissue and is described clinically as a subarachnoid hemorrhage. Hemorrhage induces an increase in intracranial pressure and subsequent compression of neighboring brain tissue and vessels, resulting in patient symptoms such as severe headaches and loss of consciousness accompanied by a high probability of ischemia due to reduced blood flow to the brain. Another complication of aneurysm rupture is cerebral vasospasm or a pathological constriction of major intracranial arteries, caused by their external exposure to blood deposited by the ruptured aneurysm.[136] Vasospasm is covered in more detail in Chap. 5. Other complications of ruptured intracranial aneurysms are described elsewhere.[133]

6.4.3.1 A Critical Radius for Saccular Aneurysms

A mathematical expression describing the state of aneurysm rupture in terms of the biophysical parameters, pressure, wall thickness, and elastic modulus, can be obtained from the volume distensibility, given by Eq. (6.26). Assuming that E is constant, the rate of volume expansion will increase continually with increasing pressure to the state where the denominator, i.e., $2E/R - P/h$, equals zero. At that point, dV/dP approaches infinity, and it can be reasoned, based on physical arguments, that rupture is

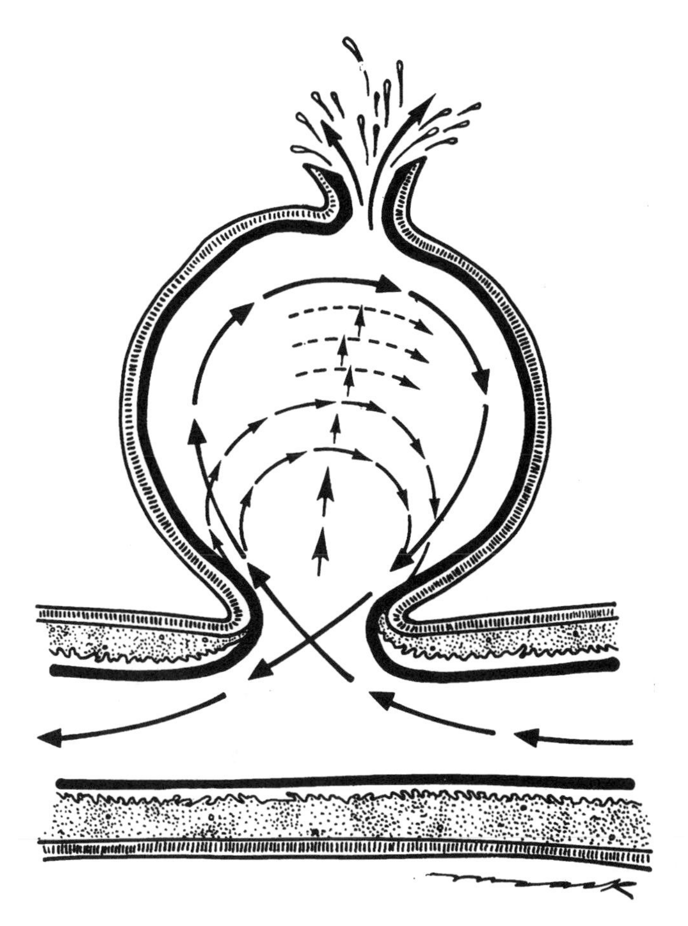

FIGURE 6.13. Schematic diagram depicting the hemodynamic patterns within a ruptured intracranial aneurysm. (Source: A.G. Osborn, Intracranial aneurysms: clinicopathologic correlations. In: *Core Curriculum Course in Neuroradiology. Part I: Vascular Lesions and Degenerative Diseases*, edited by M.N. Brant-Zawadzki, B.P. Drayer, p. 7. © 1995 by American Society of Neuroradiology.)

imminent,

$$\frac{2E}{R} = \frac{P}{h}. \tag{6.42}$$

Solving for the radius, the critical radius of the aneurysm or the size prior to rupture is

$$R_c = \frac{2Eh}{P}. \tag{6.43}$$

Figure 6.14 shows a three-dimensional graph describing the influence of h and P on the critical radius R_c. Substituting typical values of $E = 1.0$ megapascal (MPa), $h = 40\,\mu\text{m}$, and $P = 150\,\text{mm Hg}$, the critical radius is

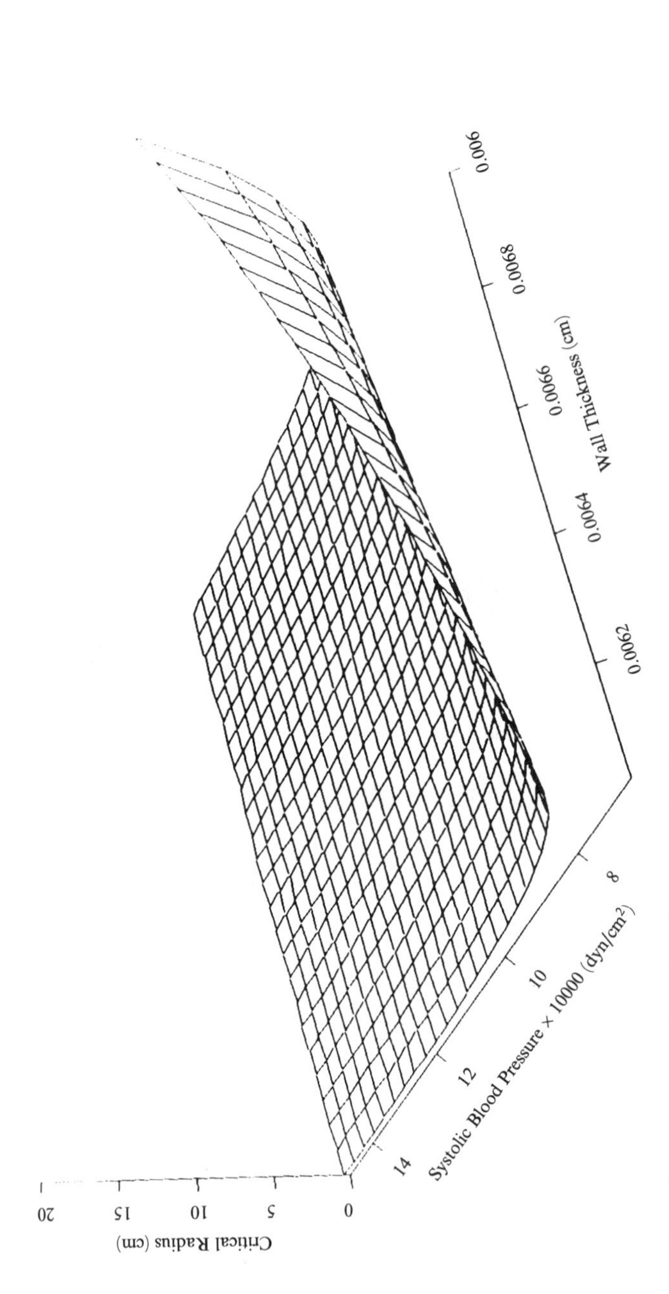

FIGURE 6.14. A three-dimensional surface plot of the critical radius of a saccular aneurysm as a function of wall thickness and systolic blood pressure over the entire range of clinically pertinent values [h: 20–60 μm; P : 6.66 × 10^4 dyn/cm^2 (50 mm Hg)–40.0 × 10^4dyn/cm^2 (300 mm Hg)] (Source: G.J. Hademenos, Neuroangiographic assessment of aneurysm stability and impending rupture based on a biomathematical model. *Neurological Research* **17**, 113–119, 1995. Reproduced by permission of the publishers Forefront Publishing.)

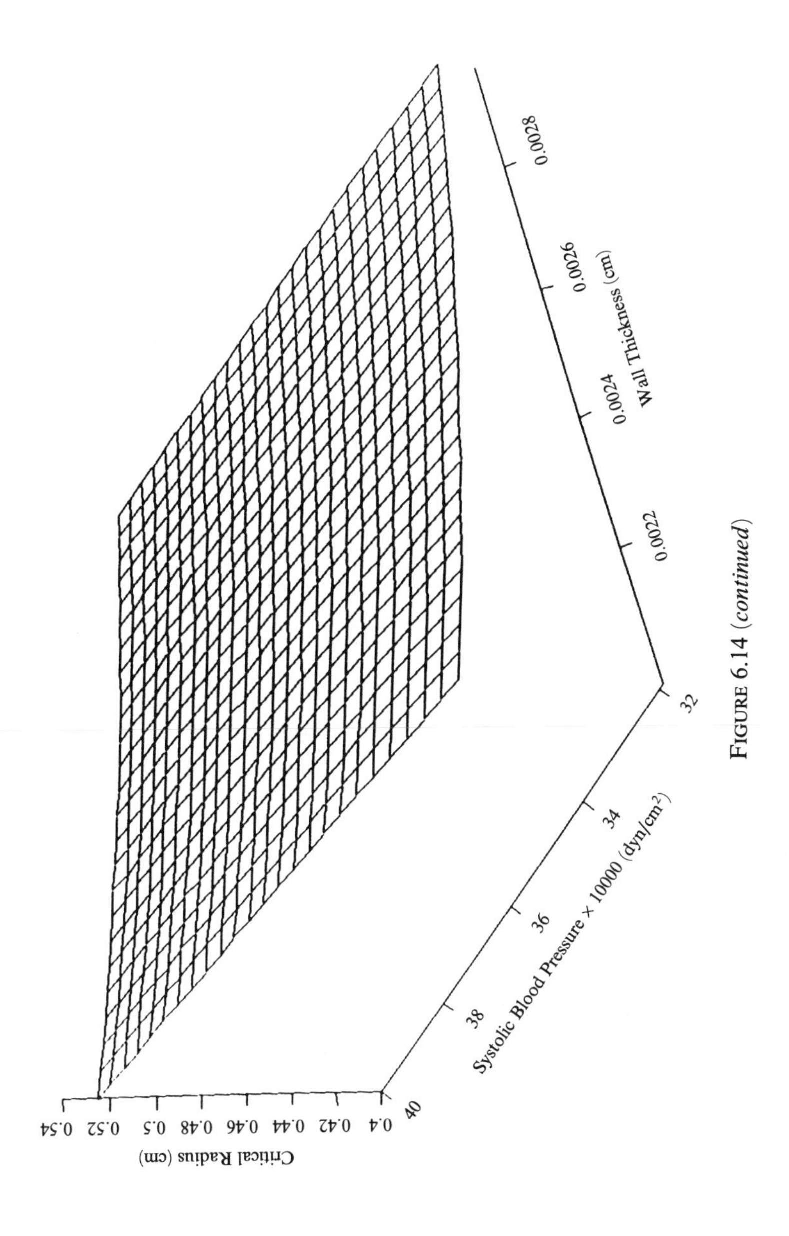

FIGURE 6.14 (*continued*)

4.0 mm. The critical radius ranges from 1.2 mm for $P = 225$ mm Hg and $E = 0.5$ MPa to 12.03 mm for $P = 100$ mm Hg and 2.0 MPa and is supported by clinical observations that the critical diameter is typically in the range 5–10 mm. Several qualitative observations can be made from the equation that describes the aneurysm prior to rupture. Any increase or decrease in the state variables that would upset this equality could possibly induce aneurysmal rupture. The critical radius increases linearly with the elastic modulus E and the wall thickness h and decreases linearly with pressure as the radius is inversely proportional to the pressure. First, it is noted that an increase in pressure results in a decrease in thickness. The static description of aneurysm growth provided by Laplace's law assumes that the amount or volume of aneurysm tissue remains constant, which is, most likely, not the case. Qualitative trends reveal a considerably large critical radius at high pressures and a slightly increasing critical radius with respect to wall thickness. One would expect that the hemodynamic forces generated by the abnormally high pressures would substantially degrade the aneurysm wall, increasing the possibility of rupture. Similar arguments can be made for the wall thickness. However, a decreasing wall thickness directly corresponds to a decrease in the collagen content, which is solely responsible at that point for the structural integrity of the aneurysm. Therefore, the weakened aneurysm wall, at a thickness of 20 μm, would be expected to rupture regardless of pressure.

6.4.3.2 The Influence of Resonance in Aneurysm Rupture

The effects of vibration have been shown to induce structural fatigue in an artery wall and are also considered to play a major role in aneurysm development.[117,118] It is believed that rupture occurs at a resonant frequency between the pulsatile hemodynamic forces and the vibrational displacement of the aneurysm wall. The detrimental effects of vibrational displacements of the artery wall have been implicated in the origin and development of cerebral aneurysms. It thus becomes interesting to consider a possible influence of vibration on the rupture of cerebral aneurysms. In other words, does a resonant frequency exist between the aneurysm wall and the pulsatile blood flow? The influence of aneurysm size on the resonant frequency of the aneurysm wall has been investigated, and an inversely proportional relationship has been observed between aneurysm radii and their corresponding frequencies. Thus, as the aneurysm radius increases, the resonant frequency decreases, supporting clinical observations that rupture is more likely for larger aneurysms. It is possible to investigate the influence of vibrational resonance on the rupture of aneurysms by using the equation of motion for an aneurysm to solve for the resonant frequency of the aneurysm wall.

In reference to the equation of motion given by Eq. (6.41), the solution ξ can be found in any elementary engineering textbook[137] and is given by

$$\xi = \frac{F_{bp}}{[(B - A\omega^2)^2]^{1/2}}. \quad (6.44)$$

The resonant frequency is the frequency determined from the maximum of Eq. (6.44), which can be rewritten as

$$\left| \frac{\xi}{F_{bp}} \right| = \frac{1}{[(B - A\omega^2)^2]^{1/2}}. \quad (6.45)$$

The maximum can be determined by squaring both sides, inverting, and differentiating with respect to ω:

$$\frac{d\left| \frac{F_{bp}}{\xi} \right|^2}{d\omega} = 2(B - A\omega^2)(-2A\omega) = 0.$$

Solving for ω, the resonant frequency due to aneurysm wall displacement can be determined approximately by[138–140]

$$\omega = \omega_{res} = \text{const} \times \frac{1}{R^2}\sqrt{\frac{ENh}{\rho_b}}, \quad (6.46)$$

where N is the neck diameter, h is the aneurysm wall thickness, R is the aneurysm radius, and ρ_b is the density of blood.

From Eq. (6.46), it now becomes possible to determine the influence of aneurysm parameters such as aneurysm radius, neck radius, and wall thickness on the resonance of the aneurysm wall. It can be seen that as the radius increases, the resonant frequency decreases, making rupture more probable. The resonant frequency increases as the elastic modulus increases (more rigid aneurysm wall) and the wall thickness increases.

Ferguson[41,121] postulated that vibrations produced as a result of hemodynamic turbulence were instrumental in the weakening of the arterial wall and the enlargement of the ensuing aneurysm. He directly measured intra-aneurysmal frequencies in patients with a phonocatheter and consistently measured musical, high-pitched bruits or tones with an average vibrational frequency of 460 ± 130 hertz (Hz). A phonocatheter is a miniature microphone that can be threaded and navigated through blood vessels to record various sounds or tones emitted by physiological processes. These measurements were performed on unruptured aneurysms, and thus aneurysm rupture could not be correlated with the observed frequency. The typical sounds of normal physiological functions emit frequencies between 20 and 200 Hz. Abnormal physiology, particularly in areas susceptible to turbulent flow such as the aneurysm emit higher frequencies typically in the range of 300–600 KHz. Another method of detecting these unique sounds or tones is the application of a specially designed acoustic stethoscope or transducer that is placed over the eye and records and analyzes intracranial blood flow sounds.[141–143] Kurokawa, Abiko, and Watanabe,[141] detected a mean frequency of 448 ± 230 Hz in 12 of 15 patients with confirmed aneurysms, while Wasserman and co-workers[142,143] detected unique spectral peaks well within the range of frequencies detected by Ferguson.

Although vibrations tend to degrade the wall and accelerate the developmental processes of the aneurysm, the occurrence of aneurysm rupture as a direct result of vibrational resonance is highly unlikely due to wide discrepancies in the frequencies of naturally occurring hemodynamic processes. It is entirely possible that the influence of vibrational displacement and resonance could serve as a secondary or supplementary role to the previously mentioned factors of wall thinning, increase in radius, and structural fatigue to precipitate aneurysm rupture. Since aneurysm rupture is extremely difficult to predict, the application of biomathematical models and *in vitro* experiments could help neurosurgeons and neuroradiologists to understand the biophysical and physiological events preceding rupture and assist in the implementation of therapeutic strategies.

6.5 Fusiform Aneurysms

Fusiform aneurysms are ellipsoidal or football-shaped aneurysms that involve the uniform circumferential ballooning of an entire segment of artery instead of a localized region as is common with the saccular aneurysms (Fig. 6.15). They are much less frequent than saccular aneurysms in the cerebrovasculature but represent the most common form of aneurysm found in the human body: abdominal aortic aneurysm. Abdominal aortic aneurysms are aneurysms that develop along the largest vessel in the human body (the aorta) in the abdominal or gut region. Fusiform aneurysms are believed to occur primarily as a result of atherosclerotic lesions that create an asymmetry in the vessel geometry. Atherosclerotic lesions are plaque calcifications or fatty deposits that accumulate along the vessel wall. They are recognized more commonly as the culprit in coronary artery disease by the term *hardening of the arteries*. The presence of atherosclerotic lesions produces a reduction in the vessel diameter, which, in turn, promotes abnormal hemodynamics. The abnormal hemodynamics are believed to be responsible for the dilatation or pouching of the vessel wall that occurs just past the lesion. These lesions are referred to as post-stenotic dilatations. Several factors may contribute to the development of post-stenotic dilatations, including (1) the conversion of the high kinetic energy of the swiftly moving bloodstream into high potential energy or lateral pressure; (2) shocks of impacts of alternating high and low pressure; (3) the increase in lateral pressure caused by the lower velocity due to the widening of the vessel, according to the Bernoulli equation; and (4) high-frequency pressure fluctuations within a turbulent field.

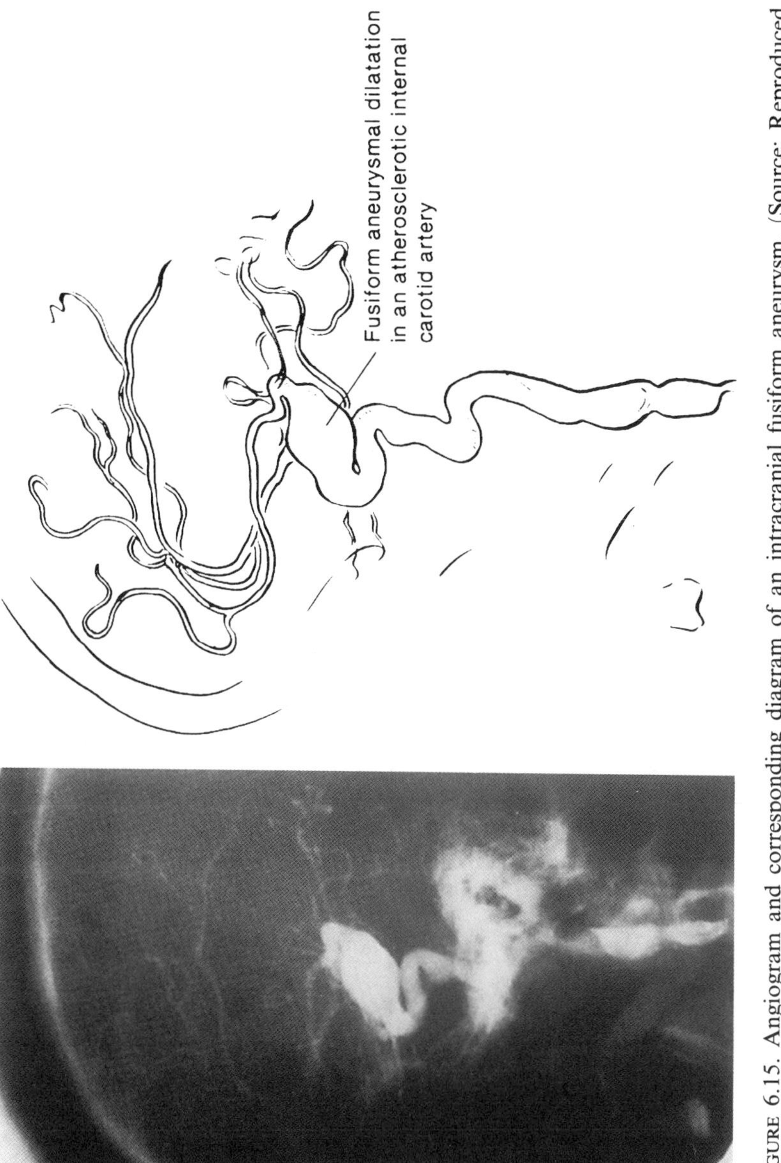

FIGURE 6.15. Angiogram and corresponding diagram of an intracranial fusiform aneurysm. (Source: Reproduced, with permission, from J.F. Toole, *Cerebrovascular Disorders*, fourth edition, 1990, p. 267. New York: Raven Press.)

6.5.1 Initiation and Development of Fusiform Aneurysms

Although they develop as sacculations along the lateral side of the arterial wall, fusiform aneurysms can be studied biomechanically through geometric extensions of the mathematical equations derived for the saccular aneurysms. The fusiform aneurysm, shown in Fig. 6.16, is a uniform ellipsoidal saccular dilatation along the lateral side of a diseased arterial segment and was modeled as a thin-walled ellipsoidal shell with a major axis radius R_a, minor axis radius R_b, circumferential tension S_θ, with θ defining the circumferential angle, meridional tension S_ϕ, with ϕ defining the meridional angle or angle with respect to the surface normal, internal saccular pressure P and uniform wall thickness, h.[144] The parameters L_θ and L_ϕ represent the original lengths of arterial wall in the unstressed state in the circumferential and meridional directions, respectively.

Laplace's law describes the distribution of forces acting on the aneurysm in static equilibrium. The force produced by the distending pressure and increasing radius is compensated by an equal and opposite force (stress) acting to resist the mechanical load placed on the aneurysm wall. The elastic ellipsoidal shell experiences stress in both the circumferential and meridional directions as both axis radii, R_a and R_b, increase. With respect to the ellipsoid, the circumferential direction is in the y axis or vertical plane and the meridional direction is in the x axis or horizontal plane. The linear expressions

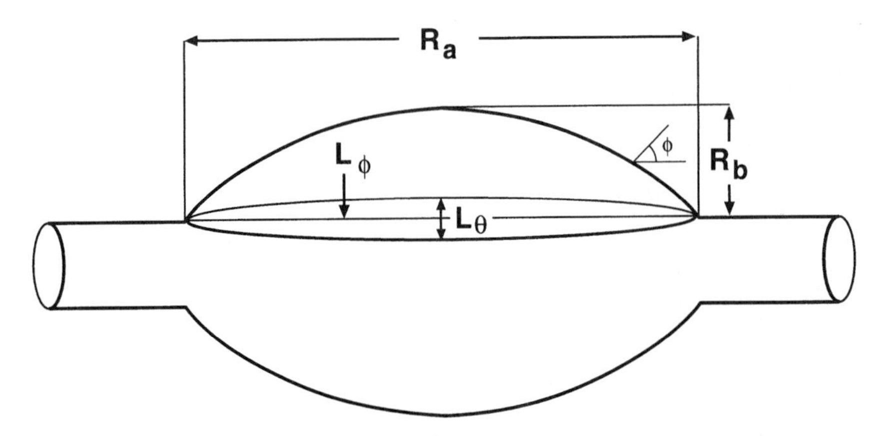

FIGURE 6.16. Schematic diagram showing the geometrical components of a fully developed fusiform aneurysm within a localized diseased region of an arterial segment. R_a represents the radius along the major axis; R_b, radius along the minor axis; L_ϕ, L_θ, the unstressed lengths of artery along the meridional and circumferential directions, respectively; ϕ is the angle describing the surface normal. (Source: G.J. Hademenos, T.F. Massoud, D.J. Valentino, G.R. Duckwiler, and F. Viñuela. A non-linear mathematical model for the development and rupture of intracranial fusiform aneurysms. *Neurological Research* **16**, 433–438, 1994. Reproduced by permission of the publishers Forefront Publishing.)

for the circumferential and meridional components of the stress are, respectively,[67,90,144]

$$S_\theta = \frac{PR_b^2}{2R_a^2 h} \frac{R_a^2 - (R_b^2 - R_a^2)\sin\phi}{(R_b^2 \sin^2\phi + R_a^2 \cos^2\phi)^{1/2}}, \tag{6.47}$$

$$S_\phi = \frac{PR_b^2}{2h} \frac{1}{(R_b^2 \sin^2\phi + R_a^2 \cos^2\phi)^{1/2}}, \tag{6.48}$$

which are, in effect, an extended representation of Laplace's law. Since rupture of the aneurysmal sac usually occurs at the fundus, is less frequent at the side, and is unlikely at the base of the aneurysm,[145] this problem is reduced to the unique case of $\phi = 90°$ (top of the aneurysm) or the point of maximum stress. Thus, the stress components given by Eqs. (6.47) and (6.48) are evaluated at $\phi = 90°$:

$$S_\theta |_{\phi=90°} = \frac{PR_b(2R_a^2 - R_b^2)}{2R_a^2 h}, \tag{6.49}$$

$$S_\phi |_{\phi=90°} = \frac{PR_b}{2h}. \tag{6.50}$$

The influence of each geometric and biophysical variable on the stress components can be seen by taking the differential of Eqs. (6.49) and (6.50):

$$dS_\theta |_{\phi=90°} = \frac{R_b(2R_a^2 - R_b^2)}{2R_a^2 h} dP - \frac{PR_b(2R_a^2 - R_b^2)}{2R_a^2 h^2} dt + \frac{P(2R_a^2 - 3R_b^2)}{2R_a^2 h} dR_b + \frac{PR_b^3}{R_a^3 h} dR_a, \tag{6.51}$$

$$dS_\phi |_{\phi=90°} = \frac{R_b}{2h} dP + \frac{P}{2h} dR_b - \frac{PR_b}{2h^2} dh. \tag{6.52}$$

The circumferential and meridional components of stress, S_θ and S_ϕ, given by Eqs. (6.47) and (6.48), are also defined as

$$S_\theta = \varepsilon_\theta E, \tag{6.53}$$

$$S_\phi = \varepsilon_\phi E, \tag{6.54}$$

where ε_θ and ε_ϕ are the components of strain along the circumferential and meridional axes, respectively, and E is the elastic modulus of the aneurysm wall. The strain can also be expressed as the ratio $\Delta R/R$, where ΔR is the change in arterial length between the relaxed and strained states and R is the length in the unstrained state as denoted by L_θ and L_ϕ. Assuming that changes in R are infinitesimal, the strain denoted in differential form is given as

$$dS_\theta = dS_\phi = \frac{dR}{R} E, \tag{6.55}$$

where

$$\frac{dR}{R} = \frac{d(R_b^2 \sin^2\phi + R_a^2 \cos^2\phi)^{1/2}}{(R_b^2 \sin^2\phi + R_a^2 \cos^2\phi)^{1/2}}$$
$$= \frac{R_b \sin^2\phi dR_b + R_a \cos^2\phi dR_a}{R_b^2 \sin^2\phi + R_a^2 \cos^2\phi}. \tag{6.56}$$

At $\phi = 90°$,

$$\left.\frac{dR}{R}\right|_{\phi=90°} = \frac{dR_b}{R_b}, \tag{6.57}$$

Therefore, equating Eqs. (6.51) and (6.52) with Eqs. (6.53) and (6.54) using Eq. (6.57) yields

$$\frac{R_b(2R_a^2 - R_b^2)}{2R_a^2 h} dP - \frac{PR_b(2R_a^2 - R_b^2)}{2R_a^2 h^2} dh + \frac{P(2R_a^2 - 3R_b^2)}{2R_a^2 h} dR_b + \frac{PR_b^3}{R_a^3 h} dR_a = \frac{E}{R_b} dR_b, \tag{6.58}$$

$$\frac{R_b}{2h} dP + \frac{P}{2h} dR_b - \frac{PR_b}{2h^2} dh = \frac{E}{R_b} dR_b. \tag{6.59}$$

Dividing both sides of Eqs. (6.58) and (6.59) by dP and solving for dR_b/dP yields

$$\left(\frac{dR_b}{dP}\right)_\theta = \left[\frac{R_b(2R_a^2 - R_b^2)}{2R_a^2 h} - \frac{PR_b(2R_a^2 - R_b^2)}{2R_a^2 h^2}\frac{dh}{dP} + \frac{PR_b^3}{R_a^3 h}\frac{dR_a}{dP}\right] \Big/ \left[\frac{E}{R_b} - \frac{P(2R_a^2 - 3R_b^2)}{2R_a^2 h}\right] \tag{6.60}$$

$$\left(\frac{dR_b}{dP}\right)_\phi = \left(\frac{R_b}{2h} - \frac{PR_b}{2h^2}\frac{dh}{dP}\right) \Big/ \left(\frac{E}{R_b} - \frac{P}{2h}\right). \tag{6.61}$$

The growth of the aneurysm can be characterized by determining the volume distensibility or rate of volume expansion, dV/dP, defined mathematically by

$$\frac{dV}{dP} = \frac{dV}{dR_b}\frac{dR_b}{dP}. \tag{6.62}$$

The volume of an ellipsoid is

$$V = \tfrac{4}{3}\pi R_a R_b^2,$$

and subsequently dV/dR_b is easily calculated:

$$\frac{dV}{dR_b} = \frac{8}{3}\pi R_a R_b.$$

Thus, the components of the volume distensibility is

$$\left(\frac{dV}{dP}\right)_\theta = \frac{8}{3}\pi R_a R_b \left(\frac{dR_b}{dP}\right)_\theta, \tag{6.63}$$

$$\left(\frac{dV}{dP}\right)_\phi = \frac{8}{3}\pi R_a R_b \left(\frac{dR_b}{dP}\right)_\phi. \tag{6.64}$$

These equations present a mathematical basis for the volumetric expansion of fusiform aneurysms. It should also be noted that fusiform aneurysms develop in a completely different manner from saccular aneurysms and are thus subject to different biomechanical parameters and functions, particularly when characterizing the critical radius for rupture.

6.5.2 *Rupture of Fusiform Aneurysms*

From a mathematical standpoint, as was the case for saccular aneurysms, rupture occurs when the denominator of the volume distensibility for each tension component approaches zero, i.e.,

$$S_\phi : \frac{E}{R_{b\phi}} = \frac{P}{2h} \quad \text{for } S_\phi, \tag{6.65}$$

$$S_\theta : \frac{E}{R_{b\theta}} = \frac{P(2R_a^2 - 3R_{\theta b}^2)}{2R_a^2 h} \quad \text{for } S_\theta. \tag{6.66}$$

The resultant critical radius can be determined from those values obtained from the individual tension components by the following:

$$R_b = [(R_{b\theta})^2 + (R_{b\phi})^2]^{1/2}. \tag{6.67}$$

The differential expressions of the volume distensibility evaluated at 90° are used to determine the critical radius of the aneurysm along the minor axis from S_θ and S_ϕ in terms of the following geometric and biophysical variables: E, the elastic modulus of the aneurysm (elastin and collagen); h, the wall thickness; P, the systolic pressure; and R_a. Using the expressions for the critical radii in terms of the stress components S_θ and S_ϕ given by Eqs. (6.65) and (6.66), the influence of biophysical and geometric variables is determined by calculating R_b while allowing the variables to vary over ranges of values observed commonly in clinical cases. Average values of $P = 150$ mm Hg, $h = 40\,\mu$m, $E = 1.0$ MPa, and $R_a = 4R_b$ yield a critical radius along the minor axis of 4.56 mm.

The critical radius decreases steadily, almost exponentially, with pressure. There is also a steady decrease in the critical radius over the range of R_a. Increases in pressure signify larger hemodynamic forces impinging upon the aneurysm wall, accelerating fatigue and imminent rupture. The pressure was defined as 150 mm Hg. It can be seen that the critical radius increases with wall thickness and decreases with R_a. An increase in wall thickness implies that the aneurysm can withstand larger increases in the radius prior to rupture. The decreases in R_a are attributed to the fact that as the ratio of major axis to minor axis increases, the aneurysm covers a wider range of area as is more susceptible to rupture at $R_a > 4R_b$, indicative of the presented data.

6.6 Clinical Assessment of Aneurysm Stability and Risk of Aneurysm Rupture

Patient mortality from the rupture of cerebral saccular aneurysms and resultant subarachnoid hemorrhage (SAH) is approximately 50% and severe neurological deficits may ensue in the remaining subset of patients who survive.[50] Although the immediate tendency is to aggressively intervene upon diagnosis of a cerebral aneurysm, the preoperative management of unruptured aneurysms has been embroiled in controversy due, in part, to the limited available data regarding the natural history of saccular aneurysms, the optimal size at which surgical intervention should be implemented, and the long-term outcomes of patients who have had operative treatment for unruptured aneurysms.[146] The aforementioned issues have fostered two distinct approaches in the management of cerebral aneurysms. The first approach is to regard the aneurysm as a potentially lethal lesion and to initiate treatment upon diagnosis, regardless of size. In the second approach, unruptured aneurysms are closely monitored until their size reaches a predefined size when treatment becomes a top priority.

In attempts to circumvent these limitations, the concept of a critical aneurysm size, based on the established observation that aneurysm rupture is highly correlated with aneurysm size,[147–149] has been introduced and generally accepted. However, the existence and value of a critical size[150] for any and all aneurysms have yet to be elucidated. Estimated values of the critical size for aneurysm rupture have ranged from 4.0 mm to >10.0 mm.[6,9,41,51,65,151–164] Given the wide variation of these published critical sizes, the following questions persist: Which value or range of critical sizes should be followed for an individual patient under observation? Is aneurysm size truly a predictor of rupture? What, if any, other descriptive aneurysm or patient parameters readily available at diagnosis are also predictive of the incidence and size of aneurysm rupture?

A critical size for aneurysmal rupture undoubtedly exists but is unlikely to be the same for each aneurysm.[165] It becomes a difficult and debatable task to pinpoint precisely a particular probability beyond which surgical intervention is necessitated. A wide range of critical size values (4 mm to >10 mm) has been proposed in the literature, making it a difficult and debatable task to pinpoint precisely a particular probability or risk of aneurysm rupture at or beyond which surgical intervention is required for a given aneurysm. More importantly, the wide variation in reported critical size values prompts one to question and ultimately reconsider the influence of aneurysm size on the incidence of rupture and its overall impact on the management of cerebral aneurysms.

Of the limited available data on the natural history of cerebral aneurysms, it has been clinically and/or experimentally documented that (1) aneurysms develop or grow at different rates,[8,47] providing substantive evidence that each aneurysm behaves in a manner unique to an individual aneurysm; (2) rupture can and does occur at any size, including small aneurysms <5 mm in diameter,[4] indicating that there exists no exclusive size or range of sizes at which rupture definitely occurs; (3) thrombosis tends to occur in larger or giant aneurysms,[59,131] particularly in those with an aneurysm size to neck size ratio of 25 : 1,[61,166] resulting in a substantially reduced risk of rupture; and (4) as an aneurysm increases in size, the aneurysm wall is more likely to contain atherosclerotic deposits along the fundus and neck,[48] changing the biomechanical stability of the aneurysm and its inherent risk of rupture. Each of these factors, either alone or in combination, could alter the developmental course of the unruptured aneurysm and thus its critical size. As a result, the risk of aneurysm rupture may not be exclusively dependent on aneurysm size, as is currently believed, and that additional descriptive patient or aneurysm factors may be predictors of rupture.[167,168]

Five clinical methods have been employed for the risk assessment of aneurysm rupture. In the first or direct approach,[51,64,157] patients presenting an unruptured aneurysm are observed and closely followed with conventional diagnostic angiography for the onset of aneurysmal SAH. The second or indirect method[150,158] assesses risk of aneurysm rupture according to aneurysms that have already ruptured and is based on the assumption that the size of the aneurysm prior to rupture is not changed significantly following rupture. Although it has not been verified experimentally or clinically, the size of a ruptured aneurysm is strongly believed to be significantly reduced from its original unruptured state and remains a valid point of criticism in discussions regarding the size of ruptured aneurysms. Yet another method used for the assessment of risk of rupture is an epidemiological method[53,169] in which the incidence of aneurysmal SAH is correlated to the prevalence of unruptured aneurysms based on a defined population according to the ratio of annual incidence rate to population at risk. The fourth method is based on decision analysis.[18,170–172] Risk assessment is performed through the application of stochastic or statistical processes to simulate the natural history of unruptured intracranial aneurysms for members from a predefined, hypothetical cohort or group of patients.

The final method for quantifying the risk of rupture of an unruptured aneurysm is the application of a biomathematical model derived from Laplace's law.[173] The critical radius of the aneurysm [Eq. (6.44)] or the radius of the aneurysm prior to rupture is obtained and described in terms of the intra-aneurysmal pressure, wall thickness, neck size, radius, and elastic modulus, each of which can either be obtained from diagnostic images or approximated sufficiently from biophysical relations. Evaluation of the risk of rupture is based on the functional distribution of the critical radius with respect to P, h, and E and is given by

$$\text{Risk} = \frac{\displaystyle\int_{P_{\min}}^{P_{\exp}} \frac{2Eh}{P}\, dP}{\displaystyle\int_{P_{\min}}^{P_{\max}} \frac{2Eh}{P}\, dP}, \tag{6.68}$$

where $P_{\min}$ and $P_{\max}$ are the minimum and maximum values of the P incorporated into the model, respectively, and $P_{\exp}$ is the systolic blood pressure of the patient determined upon clinical examination. Typically, $P_{\min} = 6.66 \times 10^4$ dyn/cm^2 (50 mm Hg) and $P_{\max} = 40.0 \times 10^4$ dyn/cm^2 (300 mm Hg). The wall thickness h and elastic modulus E of the aneurysm cannot be measured directly from angiographic images but can be approximated by the following average physiological values obtained from biomechanical experimentation of post-mortem specimens: $t = 50\,\mu$m and $E = 1.0$ MPa. Evaluation of the integrals yields the following expression for risk of aneurysm rupture:

$$\text{Risk} = \frac{\ln\left(\dfrac{P_{\exp}}{P_{\min}}\right)}{\ln\left(\dfrac{P_{\max}}{P_{\min}}\right)}, \tag{6.69}$$

This method of risk assessment of aneurysm rupture describes clinical observations based on physical reasoning. As the systolic blood pressure of the patient increases, so does the force striking the aneurysm wall, accelerating fatigue and the probability of rupture. It is highly likely that the risk of aneurysm rupture is not dependent uniquely on systolic blood pressure[31,174] and thus requires a more complex biomathematical model that implements additional aneurysm parameters. Although it remains the subject of numerous research endeavors, the ability to clinically predict aneurysm rupture, in actuality, remains highly improbable due to the uniqueness and biological complexity of each diagnosed aneurysm.[175,176]

6.7 Diagnostic Techniques for Intracranial Aneurysms

The primary objective of the neuroradiologist or neurosurgeon in the diagnosis and treatment of aneurysms is a rapid assessment of the progression and severity of the disease upon which to base decisions concerning therapy. As was stated previously, aneurysms are commonly detected only after they have either ruptured or have become fully developed. This poses a severe risk to the patient since it is unknown at what size or range of sizes that aneurysms are prone to rupture. Once an aneurysm is suspected or diagnosed at angiography, several imaging modalities or techniques such as computed tomography (CT), magnetic resonance imaging and angiography (MRI and MRA, respectively), and ultrasound (US) imaging exist from which the neuroradiologist can further elucidate the size, shape, and location of the aneurysm and begin to discuss therapeutic options.[46] The imaging technique considered the gold standard in the initial diagnosis of intracranial aneurysms is digital subtraction angiography (DSA). Briefly, DSA is a form of digital radiography that involves the use of iodinated contrast agent for the visualization of vascular anatomy. One aspect of the DSA imaging process that is important in the diagnosis of aneurysms is the sharp increase of injection pressure needed to advance the contrast agent into the vasculature has been shown, albeit rare, to be sufficient to induce aneurysm rupture.[177] Although DSA provides a relatively quick and efficient means for the diagnosis of aneurysms, the acquired images are two-dimensional projections of the aneurysm and place strict limitations as to the precise determination of geometry and the presence or size of the aneurysm lumen or neck. These factors, particularly identification of the aneurysm neck, are crucial in decisions regarding therapy. Thus, in some cases, the aneurysm arises from complex vascular geometry that may be elucidated with imaging techniques that are of sufficient resolution to detect aneurysms greater than 0.5 mm and that are capable of producing three-dimensional (3D) geometry, i.e., MRA[2,178,179] and CT angiography (CTA).[180–184]

The clinical evaluation of these techniques such as MRA and CTA is critically important in the initial diagnosis and management of patients with aneurysms. Magnetic resonance of an unclotted portion of an aneurysm reveals a negative flow defect or signal void in the lumen of the parent vessel because of the flowing blood while any clotted or thrombosed portion of an aneurysm appears as an area of decreased signal intensity.[185] This is shown in Fig. 6.17. The CT appearance of an aneurysm is a rounded area of hyperdensity in close proximity to the circle of Willis.[186] Ideally, the prospective patient would benefit tremendously from frequent and in-depth imaging examinations using both CT and MRI in addition to DSA. However, the time, cost, and availability of these imaging procedures severely restrict the use of these techniques for all patient cases. These imaging techniques and corresponding physical principles of operation are explained in detail in references cited at the end of this chapter and Chaps. 5 and 7.

6.8 Treatments for Intracranial Aneurysms

In the management of intracranial aneurysms, therapy must be considered immediately and implemented aggressively to reduce the risk of rupture. Decisions involving therapy are based on a number of factors including the general medical condition of the patient, location of the aneurysm, size of the aneurysm, growth rate of the aneurysm, the presence of multiple aneurysms, and the life expectancy of the patient.[187] The primary objective of

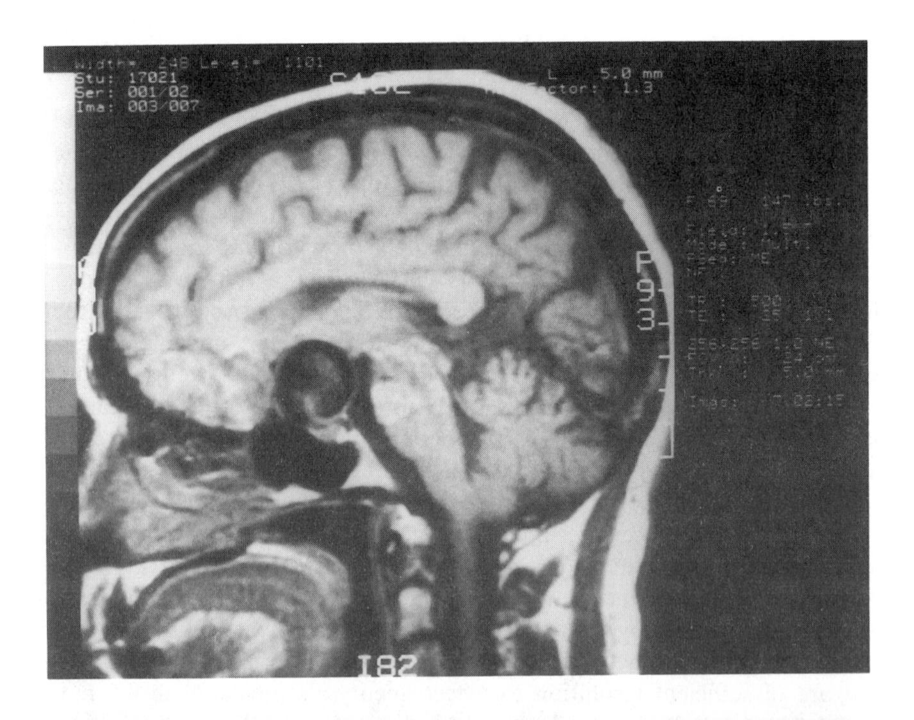

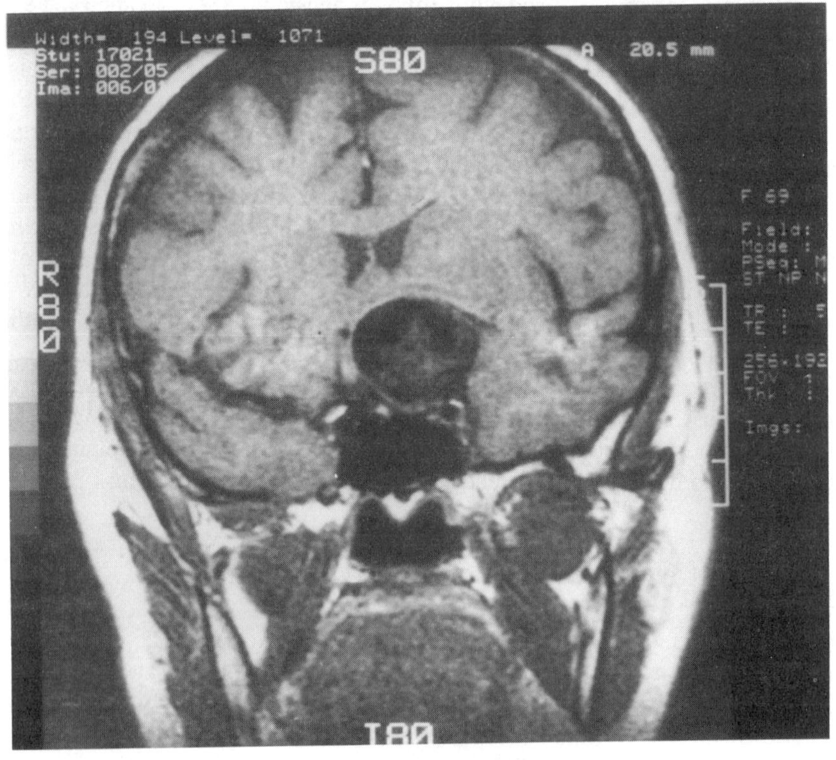

FIGURE 6.17. Computed tomographic and magnetic resonance images of an intracranial aneurysm.

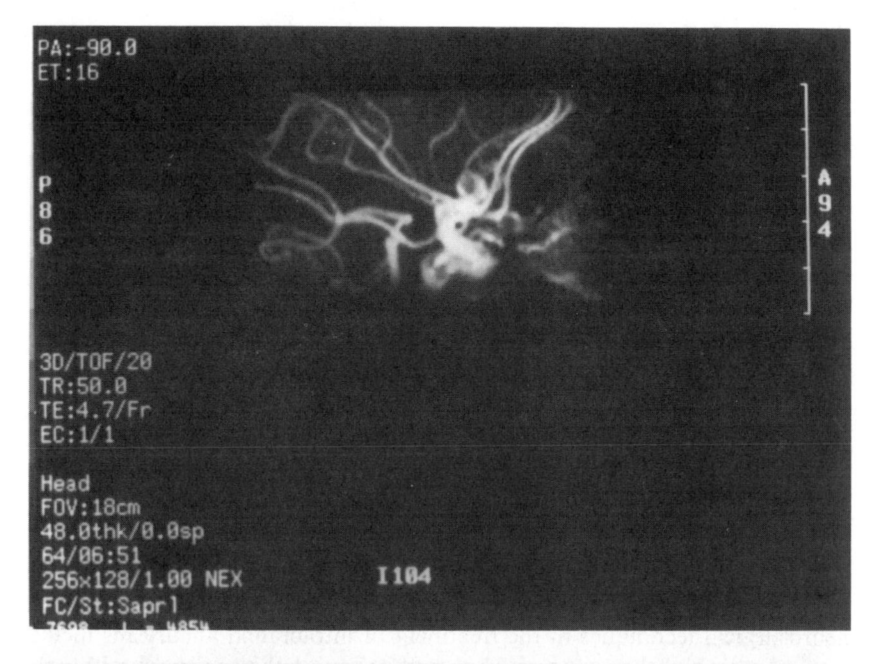

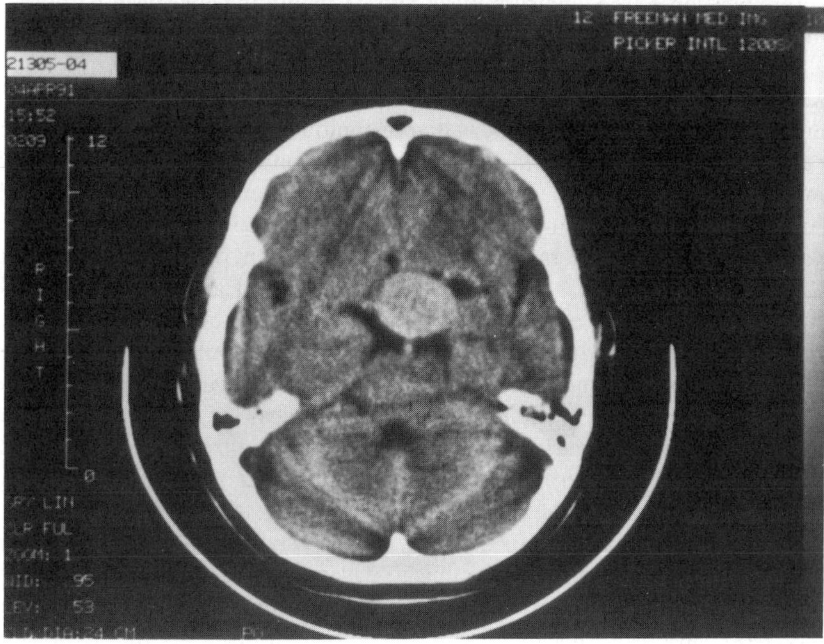

FIGURE 6.17 (*continued*)

therapeutic techniques designed to accomplish such a task is to protect the structurally fatigued aneurysm wall by securing the aneurysm neck or lumen and minimizing the effects of the hemodynamic forces and further damage. This can be accomplished through either (1) neurosurgical intervention or (2) endovascular occlusion or packing the aneurysm with mechanical agents via catheters guided through the major blood vessels. Neurosurgical intervention is the primary therapy of choice for the majority of aneurysms but is the more invasive of the procedures.[50,54] It involves direct entrance into the cranial cavity and securing of the aneurysm base or neck by clamping it with a metal clip[188] so that blood flow is, once again, redirected through the parent artery into the daughter arteries without imposing further damage to the aneurysm wall. The metal clip is applied to the base of the aneurysm, tightly closing the aneurysm neck. In addition to the problems that can be associated with an invasive surgical procedure, incomplete clipping of the aneurysm, although rare, can occur, gradually exposing a portion of the aneurysm wall referred to as a residual neck to further stresses from the hemodynamic forces imposed by the blood flow in the parent vessel.[189,190] This promotes the development of an additional or daughter aneurysm that poses similar risks of rupture and must, therefore, be treated as well. Other neurosurgical techniques in the treatment of intracranial aneurysms include suture ligation of the aneurysm neck and wrapping the aneurysm with polymerizing materials.[50]

Compared to conventional neurosurgery, endovascular embolization is a relatively newer form of therapy that is reserved typically for problematic aneurysms, inaccessible by alternative techniques. Indications for endovascular treatment include prior surgical exploration of an aneurysm with an inability to clip the neck, anatomic locations that are difficult to approach surgically, fusiform aneurysms without a well-defined neck, inability of the patient to tolerate general anesthesia, patients with poor collateral circulation for whom bypass surgery is not possible, and aneurysms with high surgical risk because of their size or location.[191] Embolization is a minimally invasive procedure where the aneurysm is embolized or filled, preventing bloodstream impingement upon the aneurysm wall.[192] Embolization can be performed using either mechanical, physical, or chemical agents to totally occlude the aneurysm. In any event, the embolization agent is transported and delivered to the aneurysm via a catheter that can be threaded from a distant accessible point in the body, e.g., the groin, and guided through the major arteries of the body all the way up to the aneurysm. An underlying factor common to clinical advances in endovascular therapy of intracranial aneurysms has been the implementation of novel strategies based on various forms of energy and energy transfer to the aneurysm, which can be accomplished by two different approaches: (1) Alteration of hemodynamics by redirecting blood flow through the parent vessel or reducing the resultant forces supplied by the hemodynamics: Examples of this approach include the use of intravascular stents (currently in preclinical phases of study) and the induction of local or systemic hypotension. Intravascular stents are cylindrical wire meshes typically constructed from a flexible, pliable material to facilitate delivery and placement in a parent vessel across an aneurysm neck.[193,194] Induction of localized or systemic hypotension involves occlusion of the parent artery proximal to an aneurysm, e.g., by permanent placement of an inflated balloon or the administration of a wide range of pharmacological agents to reduce the blood pressure and hence the effects of the hemodynamic forces on the aneurysm wall. (2) Total occlusion of the aneurysm by packing the aneurysm with mechanical agents and inducing thrombosis: This is the most widely implemented and effective of all the endovascular approaches and includes the use of mechanical agents such as balloons,[100,195–197] electrolytically detachable coils (GDCs),[198,199] mechanically detachable coils,[200–202] physical agents such as RF probes,[203–206] laser light,[207–210] and chemical agents such as biocompatible adhesives[211–216] and magnetically controlled compounds.[217,218] Figures 6.18 and 6.19 illustrate the general underlying principles of several of these therapies. As with any experimental technique or procedure, in addition to accomplishing their primary objective of occluding the aneurysm, there exist disadvantages that, in most cases, may translate into serious complications and make them unsuitable for clinical practice. Consider the previously mentioned balloon technique for aneurysm embolization. Intra-aneurysmal hemodynamics is highly irregular, forming jets upon passage from the neck or aneurysm lumen into the aneurysm dome or fundus.[219] Success of balloon embolization, first and foremost, depends on the proper timing of inflation. If inflated too soon, the balloon could cause a substantial increase of pressure within the aneurysm, inducing premature rupture. Another potential complication of balloon embolization is the possible occurrence of the water-hammer effect,[220] caused by the sudden interruption of intra-aneurysmal flow. The consequences of the water-hammer effect include enlargement of the aneurysm and possible aneurysm rupture.

At the University of California at Los Angeles and other major medical centers, the prevailing form of endovascular treatment for cerebral aneurysms is a procedure in which platinum coils (GDCs) are guided into the aneurysm through major blood vessels using a catheter.[198,199] Electric current is then applied to the coils, causing the coils to detach in the aneurysm and the blood within the aneurysm to thrombose or clot. The aneurysm is thus "packed" with the clot, which acts to protect the stressed aneurysm wall from further hemodynamic damage and imminent rupture. The results of this procedure applied to a patient with a cerebral aneurysm are shown in Fig. 6.20. Patient outcome following this procedure has been extremely encouraging and research is currently under way to further improve this technique from both a technical and a clinical standpoint.

Although not a formal method of aneurysm therapy, pharmacological regimen of hypotensive agents consists of a variety of medications designed to reduce the patient's systemic blood pressure and has been shown to

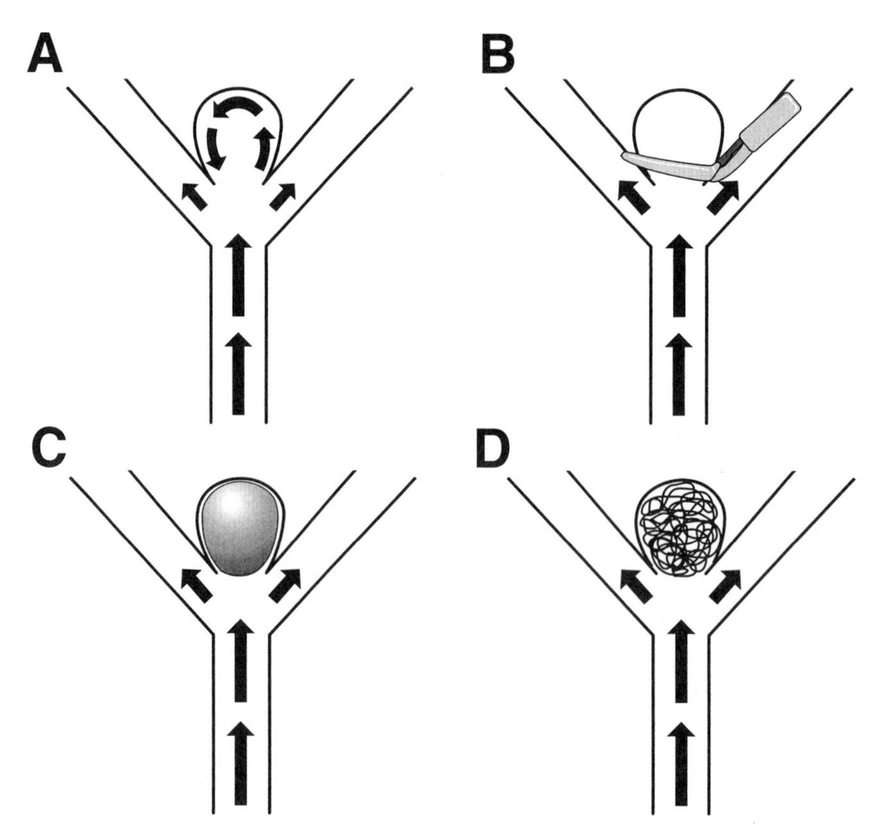

FIGURE 6.18. Schematic diagram representing the general biophysical interactions exerted by various occlusion therapies on the hemodynamics. (A) Aneurysm, untreated. (B) Aneurysm, treated by a metal clip. (C) Aneurysm, treated by a balloon. (D) Aneurysm, treated by platinum coils.

decrease effectively the probability of rupture and subsequent episodes of rerupture.[221,222] However, this represents a short-term solution to the problem since these pharmacological agents reduce the blood pressure in normotensive patients by only several mm Hg. Also, other biological or biochemical systems could act, in principle, to increase the blood pressure even under the influence of medication and increase the probability of rupture.

A novel and potential major advancement in the diagnosis and therapeutic planning of cerebral aneurysms is the application and implementation of virtual reality. Virtual reality is a collection of interface technologies that increases the ability of the user to interact with data.[223] Using specially designed software and a head-mounted display, the neurosurgeon or neuroradiologist cannot only display the aneurysm in three dimensions but can visually interact with the aneurysm by moving through any point in

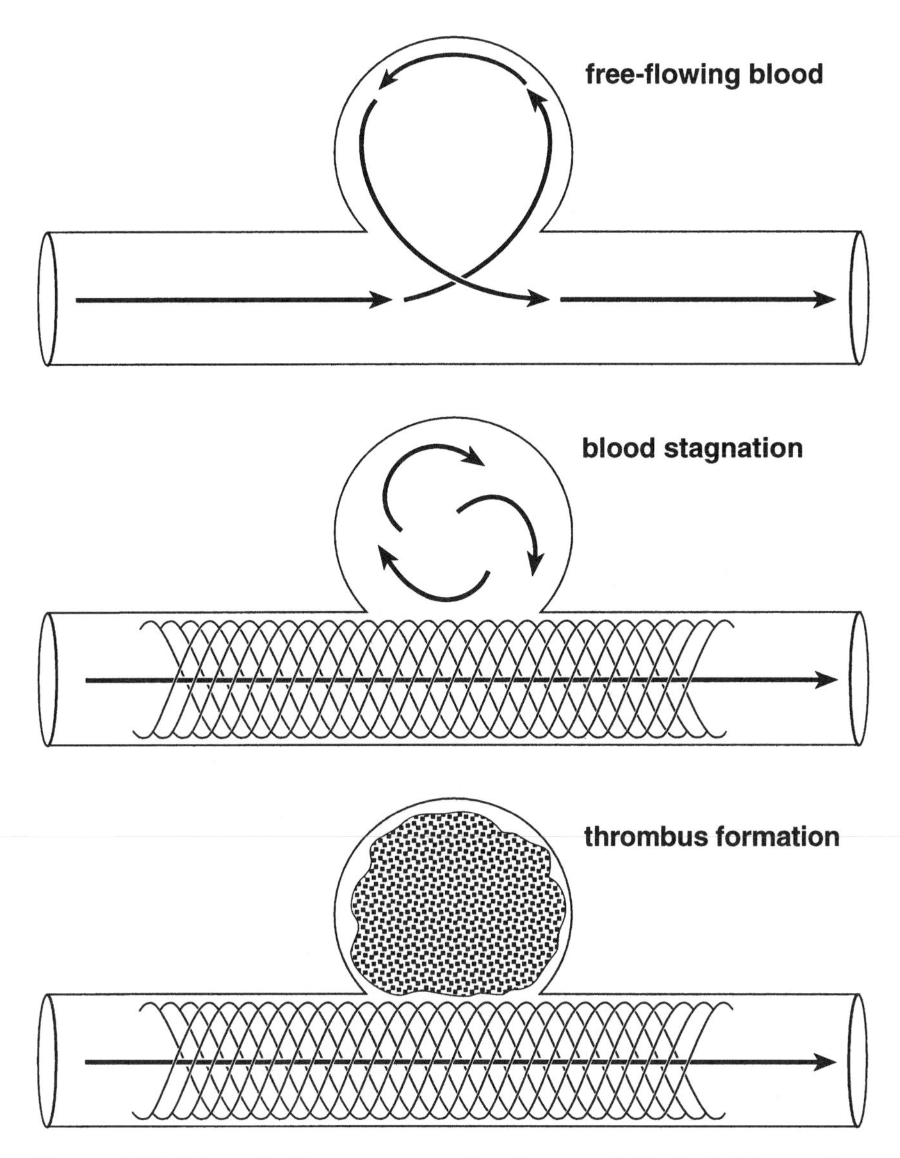

FIGURE 6.19. Schematic diagram representing the general biophysical interactions exerted by an intravascular stent on the hemodynamics.

space and acquiring views at any angle in real time. Figure 6.21 shows a three-dimensional image of an intracranial aneurysm from a swine model displayed in a virtual reality environment. It thus becomes possible to "enter" into the aneurysm through the parent vessel and assess therapeutic options. Using the three-dimensional image dataset as geometric boundaries for numerical simulations, one can also ascertain the three-dimensional distri-

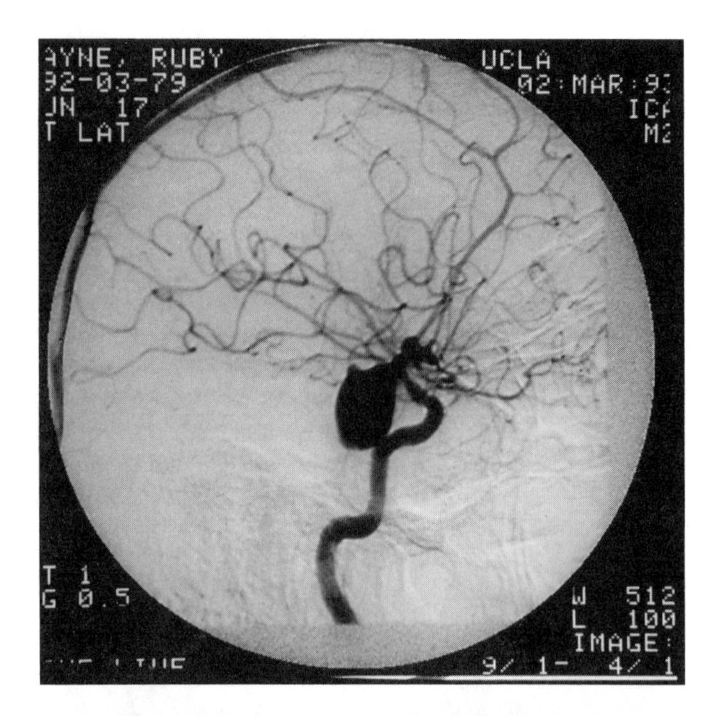

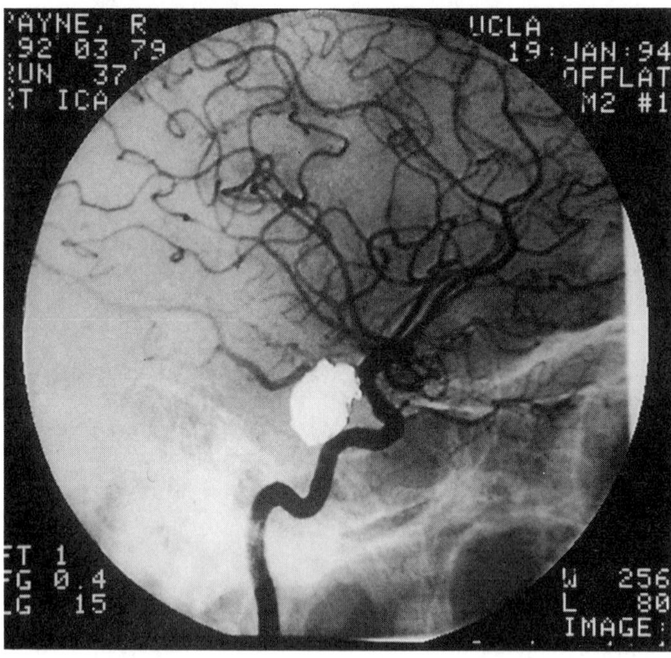

FIGURE 6.20. Digital subtraction angiography radiographic projections of the cerebrovasculature of a patient with a cerebral aneurysm (a) at diagnosis and (b) following successful endovascular therapy with electrolytically detachable coils as is evident by the complete packing of the aneurysm. (Reprinted, with permission, from G.J. Hademenos, The physics of cerebral aneurysms, *Physics Today* **48**, 24–30, 1995.)

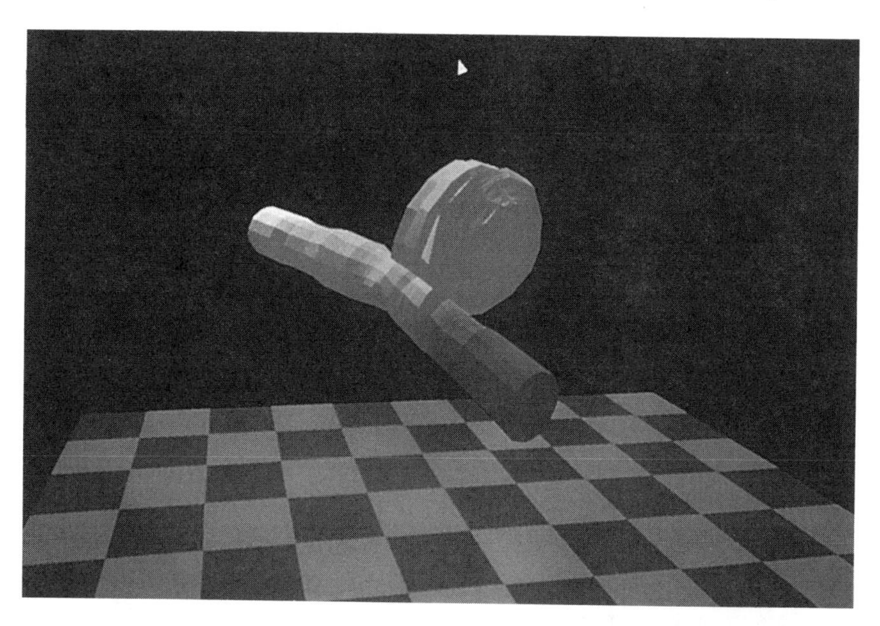

FIGURE 6.21. Three-dimensional image of an experimentally created cerebral aneurysm in a swine model reconstructed from a sequence of digital subtraction angiography projection radiographs and displayed in a virtual reality environment. The dimension provided by the colors (see also color insert that follows p. 170) reveals the relative pressure distribution determined from numerical simulation. Red represents maximum values of pressure while blue represents minimum values of pressure. (Reprinted, with permission, from G.J. Hademenos, The physics of cerebral aneurysms, *Physics Today* **48**, 24–30, 1995.)

bution of pressure and blood flow and utilize this hemodynamic information to simulate and plan therapeutic procedures and predict the outcome before interacting with the patient.

6.9 Summary

The immense complexity of blood flow hemodynamics and its role in the development of cerebral aneurysms cannot be overstated. From a theoretical standpoint, the proper characterization of the simple case of blood flow through a normal artery involves the pulsatile flow of a non-Newtonian fluid through a tapered, viscoelastic tube and requires the solution of a time-dependent nonlinear partial differential equation with variable boundary conditions. Thus, in order to acquire a qualitative and, to a lesser extent, quantitative understanding of the hemodynamic processes involved in aneurysm development, one must employ the elementary principles of physics. The influence of physical principles and interactions in each stage of the developmental process of the cerebral aneurysm in addition to diagnostic methods and therapeutic treatment is evident and remains a fundamental basis upon which to gain further knowledge and insight into this form of cerebrovascular disease. Advancing technology will provide the necessary tools for the ability to solve or approximate the appropriate differential equations, to construct elaborate and more realistic *in vitro* phantoms, and to accurately measure physical parameters leading to a more advanced understanding of how and why cerebral aneurysms occur.

However, an aneurysm presents a much more complex scenario than a simple blood vessel, with a number of factors believed to have significant roles in its origin, development, and rupture. There exists a vast number of possible factors such as genetics, biochemical disorders of collagen metabolism, immature collagen, enzymatic destruction of the arterial tissue, and preexisting health conditions such as hypertension, obesity, and diabetes. It should also be mentioned that aneurysm rupture can occur as a direct result of illicit drugs, i.e., cocaine or crack, regardless of the natural history of the aneurysm.[224–226] Research has been active particularly in the therapeutic treatment of aneurysms and, with the continuing knowledge of the physics and hemodynamics involved in each stage of aneurysm development, will improve substantially the outcome and overall quality of life of patients with cerebral aneurysms.

6.10 References

1. S. Nag and D.M. Robertson, "Gross pathologic anatomy," in *Cerebral Blood Flow: Physiologic and Clinical Aspects.* edited by J.I.I. Wood (McGraw-Hill, New York, 1987), pp. 62 and 63.
2. J.S. Ross, T.J. Masaryk, M.T. Modic, P.M. Ruggieri, E.M. Haacke, and W.R. Selman, "Intracranial aneurysms: Evaluation by MR angiography," Amer. J. Neuroradiol. **11**, 449–456 (1990).
3. P.M. Ruggieri, T.J. Masaryk, I.S. Ross, and M.T. Modic, "Intracranial magnetic resonance angiography," Cardiovasc. Intervent. Radiol. **15**, 71–81 (1992).
4. L.N. Sekhar and R.C. Heros, "Origin, growth, and rupture of saccular aneurysms: A review," Neurosurgery **8**, 248–260 (1981).
5. R. Deruty, I. Pelissou-Guyotat, C. Mottolese, and D. Amat, "Management of unruptured cerebral aneurysms," Neurol. Res. **18**, 39–44 (1996).
6. D.O. Wiebers, J.P. Whisnant, and W.M. O'Fallon, "The natural history of unruptured intracranial aneurysms," N. Engl. J. Med. **304**, 696–698 (1981).
7. G.W. Sypert, "Intracranial aneurysms: Natural history and surgical management," Compr. Ther. **4**, 64–73 (1978).
8. G.H. du Boulay, "Some observations on the natural history of intracranial aneurysms," Br. J. Radiol. **38**, 721–757 (1965).
9. T. Crawford, "Some observations on the pathogenesis and natural history of intracranial aneurysms," J. Neurol. Neurosurg. Psychiatry **22**, 259–266 (1959).
10. J.L. Chason, and W.M. Hindman, "Berry aneurysms of the circle of Willis: Results of a planned autopsy study," Neurology **8**, 41–44 (1958).

11. O. Hassler, "Media defects in human arteries," Angiology **14**, 368–371 (1963).
12. R. Leblanc, D. Melanson, D. Tampieri, and R.D. Guttmann, "Familial cerebral aneurysms: A study of 13 families," Neurosurgery **37**, 633–639 (1995).
13. A. Ronkainen, J. Hernesniemi, and G. Tromp, "Special features of familial intracranial aneurysms: Report of 215 familial aneurysms," Neurosurgery **37**, 43–47 (1995).
14. W.I. Schievink, D.J. Schaid, H.M. Rogers, D.G. Piepgras, and V.V. Michels, "On the inheritance of intracranial aneurysms," Stroke **25**, 2028–2037 (1994).
15. H.W.M. ter Berg, D.W.J. Dippel, M. Limburg, W.I. Schievink, and J. van Gijn, "Familial intracranial aneurysms: A review," Stroke **23**, 1024–1030 (1992).
16. Ö. Norrgård, K.A. Ängquist, H. Fodstad H, Å. Forsell, and M. Lindberg, "Intracranial aneurysms and heredity," Neurosurgery **20**, 236–239 (1987).
17. D.W.J. Dippel, J.W.M. ter Berg, and J.D.F. Hablena, "Screening for unruptured familial intracranial aneurysms: A decision analysis," Acta Neurol. Scand. **86**, 381–389 (1992).
18. R. Leblanc, K.J. Worsley, D. Melanson, and D. Tampieri, "Angiographic screening and elective surgery of familial cerebral aneurysms: A decision analysis," Neurosurgery **35**, 9–19 (1994).
19. R.S. Maurice-Williams, *Subarachnoid Hemorrhage: Aneurysms and Vascular Malformations of the Central Nervous System* (Wright, Bristol, 1987), p. 29.
20. I. Kanaan, P. Lasjaunias, and R. Coates, "The spectrum of intracranial aneurysms in pediatrics," Minim. Invas. Neurosurg. **38**, 1–9 (1995).
21. O. Heiskanen, "Ruptured intracranial arterial aneurysms of children and adolescents: Surgical and total management results," Child's Nerv. Syst. **5**, 66–70 (1989).
22. W.E. Stehbens, "Etiology of intracranial berry aneurysms," J. Neurosurg. **70**, 823–831 (1989).
23. D.L. Fry, "Acute vascular endothelial changes associated with increased blood velocity gradients," Circ. Res. **22**, 165–197 (1968).
24. C.M. Strother, V. Graves, and A. Rappe, "Aneurysm hemodynamics: An experimental study," Amer. J. Neuroradiol. **13**, 1089–1095 (1992).
25. S. Cajander and O. Hassler, "Enzymatic destruction of the elastic lamella at the mouth of cerebral berry aneurysms: An ultrastructural study with special regard to the elastic tissue," Acta Neurol. Scand. **53**, 171–181 (1976).
26. P. Whittaker, D.R. Boughner, and R.A. Kloner, "Role of collagen in acute myocardial infarct expansion," Circulation **84**, 2123–2134 (1991).
27. G. Neil-Dwyer, J.R. Bartlett, A.C. Nicholls, P. Narcisi, and F.M. Pope, "Collagen deficiency and ruptured cerebral aneurysms," J. Neurosurg. **59**, 16–20 (1983).
28. J.R. Østergaard and H. Oxlund, "Collagen type III deficiency in patients with rupture of intracranial saccular aneurysms," J. Neurosurg. **67**, 690–696 (1987).
29. F.M. Pope, A.C. Nicholls, P. Narcisi, J. Bartlett, G. Neil-Dwyer, and B. Doshi, "Some patients with cerebral aneurysms are deficient in type III collagen," Lancet **1**, 973–975 (1981).
30. R. Kwak, K. Mizoi, R. Katakura, and J. Suzuki, "The correlation between hypertension in past history and the incidence of cerebral aneurysms," in *Cerebral Aneurysms: Experience with 1000 Directly Operated Cases*, edited by J. Suzuki (Neuron, Tokyo, 1979), pp. 20–24.

31. W.F. McCormick and E.J. Schmalsteig, "The relationship of arterial hypertension to intracranial aneurysms," Arch. Neurol. **34**, 285–287 (1977).
32. W.E. Stehbens, "Hypertension and cerebral aneurysms," Med. J. Aust. **2**, 8–10 (1962).
33. A.E. Walker and G.W. Allegre, "The pathology and pathogenesis of cerebral aneurysms," J. Neuropath. Exp. Neurol. **13**, 248–259 (1954).
34. F.P. Handler and H.T. Blumenthal, "Inflammatory factor in pathogenesis of cerebrovascular aneurysms," J. Am. Med. Assoc. **155**, 1479–1483 (1954).
35. C.F. Gonzalez, Y.I. Cho, H.V. Ortega, and J. Moret, "Intracranial aneurysms: Flow analysis of their origin and progression," Amer. J. Neuroradiol. **13**, 181–188 (1992).
36. K.N.T. Kayembe, M, Sasahara, and F. Hazama. "Cerebral aneurysms and variations of the circle of Willis," Stroke **15**, 846–850 (1984).
37. L.E. Glynn, "Medial defects in the circle of Willis and their relation to aneurysm formation," J. Pathol. Bacteriol. **51**, 213–222 (1940).
38. D.W. Liepsch, H.J. Steiger, A. Poll, and H.-J. Reulen, "Hemodynamic stress in lateral saccular aneurysms," Biorheology **24**, 689–710 (1987).
39. G.J. Hademenos, "The physics of cerebral aneurysms," Phys. Today **48**, 24–30 (1995).
40. F. Tognetti, P. Limoni, and C. Testa, "Aneurysm growth and hemodynamic stress," Surg. Neurol. **20**, 74–78 (1983).
41. G.G. Ferguson, "Physical factors in the initiation, growth, and rupture of human intracranial saccular aneurysms," J. Neurosurg. **37**, 666–677 (1972).
42. M. Scanarini, S. Mingrino, R. Giordano, and A. Baroni, "Histological and ultrastructural study of intracranial saccular aneurysmal wall," Acta, Neurochir. (Wein) **43**, 171–182 (1978).
43. M. Scanarini, S. Mingrino, M. Zuccarello, and G. Trincia, "Scanning electron microscopy (S.E.M.) of biopsy specimens of ruptured intracranial aneurysms," Acta Neuropath. (Berl) **44**, 131–134 (1978).
44. W.E. Stehbens, "Histopathology of cerebral aneurysms," Arch. Neurol. (Chicago) **8**, 272–285 (1963).
45. E.R. Lang and M. Kidd, "Electron microscopy of human cerebral aneurysms," J. Neurosurg. **22**, 554–562 (1965).
46. E.F. Binet and E.J.C. Angtuaco, "Radiology of intracranial aneurysms," in *Neurosurgery*, edited by R.H. Wilkins and S.S. Rengachary (McGraw-Hill, New York, 1985), vol. II, pp. 1341–1354.
47. J.M. Allcock and P.B. Canham, "Angiographic study of the growth of intracranial aneurysms," J. Neurosurg. **45**, 617–621 (1976).
48. J. Suzuki and H. Ohara, "Clinicopathological study of cerebral aneurysms: Origin, rupture, repair, and growth," J. Neurosurg. **48**, 505–514 (1978).
49. G. Wilson, H.E. Riggs, and C. Rupp, "The pathologic anatomy of ruptured cerebral aneurysms," J. Neurosurg. **11**, 128–134 (1954).
50. F.B. Meyer, A. Morita, M.R. Puumala, and D.A. Nichols, "Medical and surgical management of intracranial aneurysms," Mayo. Clin. Proc. **70**, 153–172 (1995).
51. D.J. Zacks, D.B. Russell, and J.D.R. Miller, "Fortuitously discovered intracranial aneurysms," Arch. Neurol. **37**, 39–41 (1980).
52. P.D. Moyes, "Surgical treatment of multiple aneurysms and of incidentally-discovered unruptured aneurysms," J. Neurosurg. **35**, 291–295 (1971).

53. S. Dell, "Asymptomatic cerebral aneurysm: Assessment of its risk of rupture," Neurosurgery **10**, 162–166 (1982).
54. R.A. Solomon, M.E. Fink, and J. Pile-Spellman, "Surgical management of unruptured intracranial aneurysms," J. Neurosurg. **80**, 440–446 (1994).
55. M. Hayashi, S. Marukawa, H. Fujii, T. Kitano, H. Kobayashi, and S. Yamamoto, "Intracranial hypertension in patients with ruptured intracranial aneurysm," J. Neurosurg. **46**, 584–590 (1977).
56. R.J. Andrews and P.K. Spiegel, "Intracranial aneurysms. Age, sex, blood pressure, and multiplicity in an unselected series of patients," J. Neurosurg. **51**, 27–32 (1979).
57. V.K.H. Sonntag, R.H. Yuan, and B.M. Stein, "Giant intracranial aneurysms: A review of 13 cases," Surg. Neurol. **8**, 81–84 (1977).
58. T.P. Morley, and H.W.K. Burr. "Giant intracranial aneurysms: Diagnosis, course, and management," Clin. Neurosurg. **16**, 73–94 (1969).
59. M.R. Roach, "A model study of why some intracranial aneurysms thrombose but others rupture," Stroke **9**, 583–587 (1978).
60. R.L. Smith, E.F. Blick, J. Coalson, and P.D. Stein, "Thrombus production by turbulence," J. Appl. Physiol. **32**, 261–263 (1972).
61. S.P. Black and W.J. German, "Observations on the relationship between the volume and the size of the orifice of experimental aneurysms," J. Neurosurg. **17**, 984–990 (1960).
62. G.G. Ferguson, S.J. Peerless, and C.G. Drake, "Natural history of intracranial aneurysms" (Letter), N. Engl. J. Med. **305**, J 99 (1981).
63. K.K. Jain, "Mechanism of rupture of intracranial saccular aneurysms," Surgery **54**, 347–350 (1963).
64. H.B. Locksley, "Natural history of subarachnoid hemorrhage, intracranial aneurysms, and arteriovenous malformations. Based on 6,368 cases in the Cooperative Study," in *Intracranial Aneurysms and Subarachnoid Hemorrhage. A Cooperative Study*, edited by A.L. Sahs, D.W. Nibbelink, and J.C. Torner (Lippincott, Philadelphia, 1969), pp. 11–21, 37–108.
65. E. Freytag, "Fatal rupture of intracranial aneurysms: Survey of 250 medicolegal cases," Arch. Pathol. **81**, 418–424 (1966).
66. G.J. Hademenos, T. Massoud, D.J. Valentino, G. Duckwiler, and F. Viñuela, "A non-linear biomathematical model for the initiation, development, and rupture of intracranial saccular aneurysms," Neurol. Res. **16**, 376–384 (1994).
67. G.J. Hademenos, T. Massoud, D.J. Valentino, G. Duckwiler, and F. Viñuela, "A non-linear mathematical model for the development and rupture of intracranial fusiform aneurysms," Neurol. Res. **16**, 433–438 (1994).
68. N. Brown, "A mathematical model for the formation of cerebral aneurysms" Stroke **22**, 619–625 (1991).
69. P.B. Canham and G.G. Ferguson, "A mathematical model for the mechanics of saccular aneurysms," Neurosurgery **17**, 291–295 (1985).
70. E.J.-N. Hung and M.R. Botwin, "Mechanics of rupture of cerebral saccular aneurysms," J. Biomech. **8**, 385–392 (1975).
71. G. Austin, "Equation for model intracranial aneurysm with consideration of small dissipation term," Math. Biosci. **22**, 277–291 (1974).
72. J. Cronin, "Mathematical model of aneurysm of the Circle of Willis. II. A qualitative analysis of the equation of Austin," Math. Biosci. **22**, 237–275 (1974).

73. J. Duros, M.E. Clark, R.H. Kufahl, and P. Nadvornik, "On the rupture of an aneurysm," Neurol. Res. **13**, 217–223 (1991).
74. D.W. Liepsch and S.T. Moravec, "Pulsatile flow of non-Newtonian fluid in distensible models of human arteries," Biorheology **21**, 571–586 (1984).
75. K. Perktold, "On the paths of fluid particles in an axisymmetrical aneurysm," J. Biomech. **20**, 311–317 (1987).
76. K. Perktold, T. Kenner, D. Hilbert, B. Spork, and H. Florian, "Numerical blood flow analysis: Arterial bifurcation with a saccular aneurysm," Basic. Res. Cardiol. **83**, 24–31 (1988).
77. K. Perktold, K. Gruber, T. Kenner, and H. Florian, "Calculation of pulsatile flow and particle paths in an aneurysm model," Basic Res. Cardiol. **79**, 253–261 (1984).
78. S.Ø. Wille, "Pulsatile pressure and flow in an arterial aneurysm simulated in a mathematical model," J. Biomed. Eng. **3**, 153–158 (1981).
79. G.M. Austin, W. Schievink, and R. Williams, "Controlled pressure-volume factors in the enlargement of intractranial aneurysms," Neurosurgery **24**, 722–730 (1989).
80. T. Hashimoto, "Dynamic measurement of pressure and flow velocities in glass and silastic model berry aneurysms," Neurol. Res. **6**, 22–28 (1984).
81. T. Karino and M. Motomiya, "Flow visualization in isolated transparent natural blood vessels," Biorheology **20**, 119–127 (1983).
82. C.W. Kerber and C.B. Heilman, "Flow in experimental berry aneurysms: Method and model," Amer. J Neuroradiol. **4** 374–377 (1983).
83. C.W. Kerber and C.B. Heilman, "Flow dynamics in the human carotid artery: I. Preliminary observations using a transparent elastic model," Am. J. Neurol. Res. **13**, 173–180 (1992).
84. M.R. Roach, S. Scott, and G.G. Ferguson, "The hemodynamic importance of the geometry of bifurcation in the circle of Willis (glass model studies)," Stroke **3**, 255–267 (1972).
85. W.J. German and S.P.W. Black, "Experimental production of carotid aneurysms," N. Engl. J. Med. **250**, 104–106 (1954).
86. C.W. Kerber and R.W. Buschman, "Experimental carotid aneurysms: I. Simple surgical production and radiographic evaluation," Invest. Radiol. **12**, 154–157 (1977).
87. T.F. Massoud, G. Guglielmi, C. Ji, F. Viñuela, and G.R. Duckwiler, "Experimental saccular aneurysms. I. Review of surgically-constructed models and their laboratory applications," Neuroradiology **36**, 537–546 (1994).
88. T.F. Massoud, C. Ji, G. Guglielmi, F. Viñuela, and J. Robert, "Experimental models of bifurcation and terminal aneurysms: Construction techniques in swine," Amer. J. Neuroradiol. **15**, 938–944 (1994).
89. R.J. White, D.G. Fitzjerrel, and R.C. Croston, "Fundamentals of lumped compartmental modelling of the cardiovascular system," Adv. Cardiovasc. Phys. **5** (Part I), 162–184 (1983).
90. G.J. Hademenos and T.F. Massoud, "The role of the law of Laplace in the biomathematical modeling of intracranial saccular aneurysms: A review," (unpublished).
91. W. Flügge, *Stresses in Shells*, 2nd ed., (Springer, Berlin, 1973).
92. A.C. Burleson, C.M. Strother, and V.T. Turitto, "Computer modeling of intracranial saccular and lateral aneurysms for the study of their hemodynamics," Neurosurgery **37**, 774–784 (1995).

93. T. Koyama, H. Okuder, and S. Kobayashi, "Computer-assisted geometric design of cerebral aneurysms for surgical simulation," Neurosurgery **36**, 541–547 (1995).
94. B.V.R. Kumar and K.B. Naidu, "Finite element analysis of nonlinear pulsatile suspension flow dynamics in blood vessels with aneurysm," Comput. Biol. Med. **25**, 1–20 (1995).
95. A.J. Baker, *Finite Element Computational Fluid Mechanics* (Hemisphere, Washington, 1983).
96. W.E. Stehbens, *Hemodynamics and the Blood Vessel Wall* (Thomas, Springfield, III, 1979), p. 484.
97. H. Handa, N. Hashimoto, I. Nagata, and F. Hazama, "Saccular cerebral aneurysms in rats: A newly developed animal model of the disease," Stroke **14**, 857–866 (1983).
98. N. Hashimoto, H. Handa, I. Nagata, and F. Hazuma, "Experimentally induced cerebral aneurysms in rats: V. Relation of hemodynamics in the circle of Willis to formation of aneurysms," Surg. Neruol. **13**, 11–15 (1980).
99. V.B. Graves *et al.*, "Treatment of carotid artery aneurysms with platinum coils: An experimental study in dogs," Amer. J. Neuroradiol. **11**, 249–252 (1990).
100. V.B. Graves *et al.*, "Flow dynamics of lateral carotid artery aneurysms and their effects on coils and balloons: An experimental study in dogs," **13**, 189–196 (1992).
101. W.E. Stehbens, "Experimental production of aneurysms by microvascular surgery in rabbits," Vasc. Surg. **7**, 165–175 (1973).
102. J.C. White, G.P. Sayer, and J.P. Whisnant, "Experimental destruction of the media for the production of intracranial arterial aneurysms," J. Neurosurg. **18**, 741–745 (1961).
103. G.E. Tolstedt and J.W. Bell, "Production of experimental aneurysms in the canine aorta," Angiology **14**, 459–464 (1963).
104. N. Hashimoto, C. Kim, H. Kikuchi, M. Kojima, Y. Kang, and F. Hazama, "Experimental induction of cerebral aneurysms in monkeys," J. Neurosurg. **67**, 903–905 (1987).
105. M.R. Quigley, G.F. Tuite, and J.W. Cozzens, "Histology and angiography in a bifurcation aneurysm model," Surg. Neurol. **30**, 445–451 (1988).
106. D.W. Rowe, E.B. McGoodwin, G.R. Martin, and D. Grahn, "Decreased lysyl oxidase activity in the aneurysm-prone, mottled mouse," J. Biol. Chem. **252**, 939–942 (1977).
107. S. Moravec and D. Liepsch, "Flow investigations in a model of a three-dimensional human artery with Newtonian and non-Newtonian fluids. Part I," Biorheology **20**, 745–759 (1983).
108. Y.I. Cho and K.R. Kensey, "Effects of the non-Newtonian viscosity of blood on flows in a diseased arterial vessel. Part I: Steady flows," Biorheology **28**, 241–262 (1991).
109. P.B. Canham, P. Whittaker, S.E. Barwick, and M.E. Schwab, "Effect of pressure on circumferential order of adventitial collagen in human brain arteries," Can. J. Physiol. Pharmacol. **70**, 296–305 (1992).
110. R.B. Jenkins and R.W. Little, "A constitutive equation for parallel-fibred elastic tissue," J. Biomech. **7**, 397–402 (1974).
111. R.C. Haut and R.W. Little, "A constitutive equation for collagen fibers," J. Biomech. **5**, 423–430 (1972).
112. V.T. Turitto and H.L. Goldsmith, "Rheology, transport, and thrombosis in the

circulation," in Loscalzo J, Creager MA, Dzau VJ (eds.). *Vascular Medicine: A Textbook of Vascular Biology and Diseases*, edited by J. Loscalzo, M.A. Creager, and V.J. Dzau (Little, Brown, Boston, 1992), Chap. 5, pp. 157–204.

113. S. Rossitti and J. Löfgren, "Optimality principles and flow orderliness at the branching points of cerebral arteries," Stroke **24**, 1029–1032 (1993).
114. A.L. Day, "Hemodynamics, atherosclerosis, and the genesis of intracranial aneurysms," in Proceedings of the First Annual Meeting of the Joint Section on Cerebrovascular Surgery of the American Association of Neurological Surgeons and the Congress of Neurological Surgeons. Park Ridge, IL; American Association of Neurological Surgeons, 1996, pp. 49–50.
115. T.W.R. Macfarlane, P.B. Canham, and M.R. Roach, "Shape changes at the apex of isolated human cerebral bifurcations with changes in transmural pressure," Stroke **14**, 70–76 (1982).
116. W.W. Nichols and M.F. O'Rourke, *McDonald's Blood Flow in Arteries: Theoretic, Experimental and Clinical Principles* (Lea & Febiger, Philadelphia, 1990), 24–26.
117. D.R. Boughner and M.R. Roach, "Effect of low frequency vibration on the arterial wall," Circ. Res. **29**, 136–144 (1971).
118. M.R. Roach and E. Melech, "The effect of sonic vibration on isolated human iliac arteries," Can. J. Physiol. Pharmacol. **49**, 288–291 (1971).
119. P.B. Dobrin, W.H. Baker, and W.C. Gley, "Elastolytic and collagenolytic studies of arteries: Implications for the mechanical properties of aneurysms," Arch. Surg. **119**, 405–409 (1984).
120. P.B. Dobrin and R. Mrkvicka, "Failure of elastin or collagen as possible critical connective tissue alterations underlying aneurysmal dilatation," Cardiovasc. Surg. **2**, 484–488 (1994).
121. G.G. Ferguson, "Turbulence in human intracranial saccular aneurysms," J. Neurosurg. **33**, 485–497 (1970).
122. W.E. Stehbens, "Turbulence of blood flow," Quart. J. Exp. Physiol. **44**, 110–117 (1959).
123. G.G. Ferguson, "Direct measurement of mean and pulsatile blood pressure at operation in human intracranial saccular aneurysms," J. Neurosurg. **36**, 560–563 (1972).
124. L.N. Sekhar, R.J. Sclabassi, M. Sun, H.B. Blue, and J.F. Wasserman, "Intra-aneurysmal pressure measurements in experimental saccular aneurysms in dogs," Stroke **19**, 352–356 (1988).
125. A.M. Coll, J.F. del Corral, S. Yazawa, and M. Falcón, "Intra-aneurysmal pressure difference in human saccular aneurysms," Surg. Neurol. **6**, 93–96 (1976).
126. S. Scott, G.G. Ferguson, and M.R. Roach, "Comparison of the elastic properties of human intracranial arteries and aneurysms," Can. J. Physiol. Pharmacol. **50**, 328–332 (1972).
127. A.F. Zubillaga, G. Guglielmi, F. Viñuela, and G.R. Duckwiler, "Endovascular occlusion of intracranial aneurysms with electrically detachable coils: correlation of aneurysm neck size and treatment results," Amer. J. Neuroradiol. **15**, 815–820 (1994).
128. T.D. Mast and A.D. Pierce, "A theory of aneurysm sounds," J. Biomech. **28**, 1045–1053 (1995).
129. C.M. Strother, "In vitro study of hemodynamics in a giant saccular aneurysm

model: Influence of flow dynamics in the parent vessel and effects of coil embolization (Correspondence), Neuroradiology **36**, 530–536 (1994).

130. P.V. Moulder, "Physiology and biomechanics of aneurysms," in *Aneurysms*, edited by M.D. Kerstein, P.V. Moulder, and W.R. Webb (Williams & Wilkins, Baltimore, 1983), Chap. 2, p. 20.
131. C.M. Strother, "In vitro study of hemodynamics in a giant saccular aneurysm model: Influence of flow dynamics in the parent vessel and effects of coil embolization" (Letter; Comment), Neuroradiology **37**, 159–161 (1995).
132. Y.P. Gobin, J.L. Counord, P. Flaud, J. Duffaux, "In vitro study of hemodynamics in a giant saccular aneurysm model: Influence of flow dynamics in the parent vessel and effects of coil embolization," Neuroradiology **36**, 530–536 (1994).
133. R.W. Tarr, J. Perl II, and T.J. Masaryk, "Neuroradiological aspects of aneurysms," in *Ruptured Cerebral Aneurysms: Perioperative Management*, edited by R.A. Ratcheson and F.P. Wirth (Williams & Wilkins, Baltimore, 1994), Vol. 6, *Concepts in Neurosurgery*, p. 182.
134. B. Voldby, "Ruptured intracranial aneurysm: A clinical and pathophysiological study," Dan. Med. Bull. **33**, 53–64 (1986).
135. J.C. Jaeger, *Elasticity, Fracture and Flow with Engineering and Geological Applications* (Wiley, New York, 1956), pp. 85, 169–170.
136. R.H. Wilkins, "Cerebral vasospasm," in *Neurosurgery Update II: Vascular, Spinal, Pediatric, and Functional Neurosurgery*, edited by R.H. Wilkins and S.S. Rengachary (McGraw-Hill, New York, 1991), p. 78.
137. A.D. Nashif, D.I.G. Jones, and J.P. Henderson, *Vibration Damping* (Wiley, New York, 1985), p. 122.
138. A.C. Van Bruggen, "The Acoustic Detection of Intracranial Aneurysms," doctoral thesis, Rijksuniversiteit Groningen, The Netherlands (1994).
139. T.D. Mast, "Physical Theory of Narrow-Band Sounds Associated with Intracranial Aneurysms," doctoral thesis, The Pennsylvania State University (1993).
140. J.F. Wasserman, "The Acoustic Detection of Cerebral Aneurysms," doctoral thesis, The University of Cincinnati (1975).
141. Y. Kurokawa, S. Abiko, and K. Watanabe, "Noninvasive detection of intracranial vascular lesions by recording blood flow sounds," Stroke **25**, 397–402 (1994).
142. C.P. Olinger and J.F. Wasserman, "Electronic stethoscope for detection of cerebral aneurysm, vasospasm and arterial disease," Surg. Neurol. **8**, 298–312 (1977).
143. F.J. Taylor, A.S. Ramnarayan, and J. Wasserman, "Non-invasive aneurysm detection using digital signal processing," J. Biomed. Eng. **5**, 210–210. (1983).
144. D.J. Patel and R.N. Vaishnav, "Some elementary hemodynamic concepts," in *Basic Hemodynamics and Its Role in Disease Processes* (University Park, Baltimore, 1980), Chap. 2.
145. W.E. Stehbens, *Hemodynamics and the Blood Vessel Wall* (Thomas, Springfield, Ill, 1979), pp. 476–477.
146. G.A. Dix, W. Gordon, A.M. Kaufmann, I.S. Sutherland, and G.R. Sutherland, "Ruptured and unruptured intracranial aneurysms—surgical outcome," Can. J. Neurol. Sci. **22**, 187–191 (1995).
147. P. Dickey, J. Nunes, C. Bautista, and I. Goodrich, "Intracranial aneurysms:

Size, risk of rupture, and prophylactic surgical treatment," Conn. Med. **58**, 583–586 (1994).
148. L.A. Rogers, "Intracranial aneurysm size and potential for rupture" (Letter), J. Neurosurg. **67**, 475–476 (1987).
149. D.O. Wiebers, J.P. Whisnant, T.M. Sundt, Jr., and W.M. O'Fallon, "Intracranial aneurysm size and potential for rupture" (Letter), J. Neurosurg. **67**, 476 (1987).
150. J. Rosenørn and V. Eskesen, "Does a safe-size limit exist for unruptured intracranial aneurysms?" Acta Neurochir. (Wien) **121**, 113–118 (1993).
151. R.G. Ojemann, "Management of the unruptured intracranial aneurysm," N. Engl. J. Med. **304**, 725–726 (1981).
152. M.R. Crompton, "Mechanism of growth and rupture in cerebral berry aneurysms," Br. Med. J. **1**, 1138–1142 (1966).
153. N. Hashimoto and H. Handa, "The size of cerebral aneurysms in relation to repeated rupture," Surg. Neurol. **19**, 107–111 (1983).
154. S. Juvela, M. Porras, and O. Heiskanen, "Natural history of unruptured intracranial aneurysms: A long-term follow-up study," J. Neurosurg. **79**, 174–182 (1993).
155. K. Mizoi, T. Yoshimoto, Y. Nagamine, T. Kayama, and K. Koshu, "How to treat incidental cerebral aneurysms: A review of 139 consecutive cases," Surg. Neurol. **44**, 114–121 (1995).
156. K. Mizoi, R. Kwak, T. Sakamoto, and J. Suzuki, "Angiographical study of intracranial saccular aneurysms: With particular reference to their size and shape," in *Cerebral Aneurysms: Experience with 1000 Directly Operated Cases*, edited by J. Suzuki (Neuron, Tokyo, 1979), pp. 163–170.
157. D.O. Wiebers, J.P. Whisnant, T.M. Sundt, and W.M. O'Fallon, "The significance of unruptured intracranial saccular aneurysms," J. Neurosurg. **66**, 23–29 (1987).
158. W.F. McCormick and G.J. Acosta-Rua, "The size of intracranial saccular aneurysms: An autopsy study," J. Neurosurg. **33**, 422–427 (1970).
159. S. Asari and T. Ohmoto, "Natural history and risk factors of unruptured cerebral aneurysms," Clin. Neurol. Neurosurg. **95**, 205–214 (1993).
160. W.E. Stehbens, "Aneurysms and anatomical variation of cerebral arteries," Arch. Pathol. **75**, 45–64 (1963).
161. N.F. Kassell and J.C. Torner, "Size of intracranial aneurysms," Neurosurgery **12**, 291–297 (1983).
162. T. Inagawa and A. Hirano, "Ruptured intracranial aneurysms: An autopsy study of 133 patients," Surg. Neurol. **33**, 117–123 (1990).
163. T.M. Sundt, S. Kobayashi, N.C. Fode, and J.P. Whisnant, "Results and complications of surgical management of 809 intracranial aneurysms in 722 cases," J. Neurosurg. **56**, 753–765 (1982).
164. W.F. McCormick and J.D. Nofzinger, "Saccular intracranial aneurysms: An autopsy study," J. Neurosurg. **22**, 155–159 (1965).
165. W.I. Schievink, D.G. Piepgras, and F.P. Wirth, "Rupture of previously documented small asymptomatic saccular intracranial aneurysms. Report of three cases," J. Neurosurg. **76**, 1019–1024 (1992).
166. S.P.W. Black, H.-L.Leo, and W.L. Carson, "Recording and measuring the interior features of intracranial aneurysms removed at autopsy: Method and initial findings," Neurosurgery **22**, 40–44 (1988).

167. G.J. Hademenos, T.F. Massoud, and J.W. Sayre, "Anatomic and morphological factors that correlate with cerebral aneurysm rupture in patients referred for endovascular treatment," (unpublished).
168. S.M. de la Monte, G.W. Moore, M.A. Monk, and G.M. Hutching, "Risk factors for the development and rupture of intracranial berry aneurysms," Am. J. Med. **78**, 957–964 (1985).
169. J. Rosenørn, V. Eskesen, and K. Schmidt, "Unruptured intracranial aneurysms: An assessment of the annual risk of rupture based on epidemiological and clinical data," Br. J. Neurosurg. **2**, 369–378 (1988).
170. R. Leblanc and K.J. Worsley, "Surgery of unruptured, asymptomatic aneurysms: A decision analysis," Can. J. Neurol. Sci. **22**, 30–35 (1995).
171. H. van Crevel, J.D. Habbema, R. Braakman, "Decision analysis of the management of incidental intracranial saccular aneurysms," Neurology **36**, 1335–1339 (1986).
172. S.G. Pauker and J.P. Kassirer, "Decision analysis," N. Engl. J. Med. **316**, 250–258 (1987).
173. G.J. Hademenos, "Neuroangiographic assessment of aneurysm stability and impending rupture based on a biomathematical model," Neurol. Res. **17**, 113–119 (1995).
174. B.K. Dandapani, S. Suzuki, R.E. Kelley, Y. Reyes-Iglesias, and R.C. Duncan, "Relation between blood pressure and outcome in intracerebral hemorrhage," Stroke **26**, 21–24 (1995).
175. A.L. Sahs, D.W. Nibbelink, and J.C. Torner, editors, *Aneurysmal Subarachnoid Hemorrhage*, Report of the Cooperative Study (Urban & Schwarzenberg, Baltimore, 1981).
176. S. Komatsu, H. Seki, K. Uneoka, A. Takaku, and J. Suzuki, "Rupturing factors of intracranial aneurysm: Season, weather and psychsomatic strain," in *Cerebral Aneurysms: Experience with 1000 Directly Operated Cases*, edited by J. Suzuki (Neuron, Tokyo, 1979), pp. 25–31.
177. G.H. Koenig, W.H. Marshall, Jr., G.J. Poole, and R.A. Kramer, "Rupture of intracranial aneurysms during cerebral angiography: Report of ten cases and review of the literature," Neurosurgery **5**, 314–324 (1979).
178. N. Kurihara, S. Takahashi, S. Higano, K. Matsumoto, I. Yanagawa, A. Takahashi, and K. Sakamoto, "Evaluation of large intracranial aneurysm with three-dimensional MRI," J. Comput, Assist. Tomogr. **19**, 707–712 (1995).
179. J. Huston III, D.A. Nichols, P.H. Luetmer, J.T. Goodwin, F.B. Meyer, D.O. Wiebers, and A.L. Weaver, "Blinded prospective evaluation of sensitivity of MR angiography to known intracranial aneurysms: Importance of aneurysm size," Amer. J. Neuroradiol. **15**, 1607–1614 (1994).
180. R.A. Alberico, M. Patel, S. Casey, B. Jacobs, W. Maguire, and R. Decker, "Evaluation of the circle of Willis with three-dimensional CT angiography in patients with suspected intracranial aneurysms," Amer. J. Neuroradiol. **16**, 1571–1578 (1995).
181. E.Y. Liang, M. Chan, J.H.K. Hsiang, S.B. Walkden, W.S. Poon, W.W.M. Lam, and C. Metreweli, "Detection and assessment of intracranial aneurysms: Value of CT angiography with shaded-surface display," Amer. J. Roentgenol. **165**, 1497–1502 (1995).
182. E.R. Heinz, "Prospective evaluation of the circle of Willis with three-dimensional CT angiography in patients with suspected intracranial aneurysms," Amer. J. Neuroradiol. **16**, 1579–1580 (1995).

183. S. Aoki, Y. Sasaki, T. Machida, T. Ohkubo, M. Minami, and Y. Sasaki, "Cerebral aneurysms: Detection and delineation using three-dimensional CT angiography," Amer. J. Neuroradiol. **13**, 1115–1120 (1992).
184. R.K. Zeman, P.M. Silverman, P.T. Vieco, and P. Costello, "CT angiography," Amer. J. Roentgenol. **165**, 1079–1088 (1995).
185. R.G. Ramsey, "Aneurysms and vascular malformations," in *Neuroradiology*, 2nd ed., edited by R.G. Ramsey, (Saunders, Philadelphia, 1987), Chap. 6, p. 265.
186. R.W. Tarr, J. Perl II, and T.J. Masaryk, "Neuroradiological aspects of aneurysms," in *Ruptured Cerebral Aneurysms: Perioperative Management*, edited by R.A. Ratcheson and F.P. Wirth (Williams & Wilkins, Baltimore, 1994), Vol. 6: *Concepts in Neurosurgery*, p. 183.
187. J. Rosenørn and V. Eskesen, "Patients with ruptured intracranial saccular aneurysms: Clinical features and outcome according to the size," Br. J. Neurosurg. **8**, 73–78 (1994).
188. M.T. Lawton, J.C. Ho, W.D. Bichard, S.W. Coons, J.M. Zabramski, and R.F. Spetzler, "Titanium aneurysm clips: Part I—Mechanical, radiological, and biocompatibility testing," Neurosurgery **38**, 1158–1164 (1996).
189. T. Lin, A.J. Fox, and C.G. Drake, "Regrowth of aneurysm sacs from residual neck following aneurysm clipping," J. Neurosurg. **70**, 556–560 (1989).
190. C.G. Drake and R.G. Vanderlinden, "The late consequences of incomplete surgical treatment of cerebral aneurysms," J. Neurosurg. **27**, 226–238 (1967).
191. J.A. Bauzà, "Interventional neuroradiology," in *Essentials of Neurosurgery: A Guide to Clinical Practice*, edited by M.B. Allen, Jr., and R.H. Miller (McGraw-Hill, New York, 1995), Chap. 17, p. 338.
192. G. Guglielmi, "Endovascular treatment of intracranial aneurysms," Neuroimag. Clin. N. Amer. **2**, 269–278 (1992).
193. G. Geremia, M. Kaklin, and L. Brennecke, "Embolization of experimentally created aneurysms with intravascular stent devices," Amer. J. Neuroradiol. **15**, 1223–1231 (1994).
194. I. Szikora, L.R. Guterman, S.C. Standard, A.K. Wakhloo, and L.N. Hopkins, "Endovascular treatment of experimental aneurysms with liquid polymers: The protective potential of stents," Neurosurgery **38**, 339–347 (1996).
195. R.T. Higashida, V.V. Halbach, B. Dormandy, J.D. Bell, and G.B. Hieshima, "Endovascular treatment of intracranial aneurysms with a new silicone microballoon device: Technical considerations and indications for therapy," Radiology **174**, 687–691 (1990).
196. G.K. Geremia *et al.*, "Balloon embolization of experimentally created aneurysms: An animal training model," Amer. J. Neuroradiol. **11**, 659–662 (1990).
197. G. Debrun *et al.*, "Inflatable and released balloon technique experimentation in dog-application in man," Neuroradiology **9**, 267–271 (1975).
198. G. Guglielmi *et al.*, "Electrothrombosis of saccular aneurysms via endovascular approach. Part 1: Electrochemical basis, technique, and experimental results," J. Neurosurg. **75**, 1–7 (1991).
199. G. Guglielmi, F. Viñuela, J. Dion, and G. Duckwiler, "Electrothrombosis of saccular aneurysms via endovascular approach. Part 2: Preliminary clinical experience," J. Neurosurg. **75**, 8–14 (1991).
200. R.C. Dawson, A.F. Krisht, D.L. Barrow, G.J. Jospeh, G.G. Shengelaia, and G. Bonner, "Treatment of experimental aneurysms using collagen-coated microcoils," Neurosurgery **36**, 133–140 (1995).

201. R.C. Dawson III, G.G. Shengelaia, A.F. Krisht, and G.D. Bonner, "Histologic effects of collagen-filled interlocking detachable coils in the ablation of experimental aneurysms in swine," Amer. J. Neuroradiol. **17**, 853–858 (1996).
202. M.P. Marks, H. Chee, R.P. Liddell, G.K. Steinberg, N. Panahian, and B. Lane, "A mechanically detachable coil for the treatment of aneurysms and occlusion of blood vessels," Amer. J. Neuroradiol. **15**, 821–827 (1994).
203. W.S. Yamanashi *et al.*, "Electromagnetically induced focused heat in the treatment of surgically created aneurysm models," Invest. Radiol. **22**, 574–580 (1987).
204. A.A. Patil *et al.*, "Electromagnetic field focusing (EFF) probe in aneurysm thrombosis. Preliminary report," Acta Neurochir. **81**, 68–71 (1986).
205. P.N. Sawyer and J.W. Pate, "Bio-electric phenomena as an etiologic factor in intravascular thrombosis," Am. J. Physiol. **175**, 103–107 (1953).
206. P.N. Sawyer, J.W. Pate, and C.S. Weldon, "Relations of abnormal and injury electric potential differences to intravascular thrombosis," Am. J. Physiol. **175**, 108–112 (1953).
207. A. Guity *et al.*, "Mural repair following obliteration of aneurysms. Part III: Pathomorphological effects of Nd:YAG laser on aneurysm obliteration," Microsurgery **12**, 30–34 (1991).
208. G. Maira *et al.*, "Laser photocoagulation for treatment of experimental aneurysms," J. Microsurg. **1**, 137–147 (1979).
209. H.C. Zweng and M. Flocks, "Clinical experiences with laser photocoagulation," Fed. Proc. **24** (Suppl. 14), 65–70 (1965).
210. G.V. O'Reilly *et al.*, "Laser-induced thermal occlusion of berry aneurysms: Initial experimental results," Radiology **171**, 471–474 (1989).
211. S. Mandai, K. Kinugasa, and T. Ohmoto, "Direct thrombosis of aneurysms with cellulose acetate polymer. Part I: Results of thrombosis in experimental aneurysms," J. Neurosurg. **77**, 497–500 (1992).
212. T. Suga *et al.*, "Experimental study of aneurysm occlusion with fibrin glue," Neurol. Surg. **20**, 865–873 (1992).
213. G.M. Debrun *et al.*, "Obliteration of experimental aneurysms in dogs with isobutyl-cyanoacrylate," J. Neurosurg. **61**, 37–43 (1984).
214. P.H. Zanetti and F.E. Sherman, "Experimental evaluation of a tissue adhesive as an agent for the treatment of aneurysms and arteriovenous anomalies," J. Neurosurg. **36**, 72–79 (1972).
215. J.R. Moringlane *et al.*, "Occlusion of experimental artery aneurysms by intrasaccular injection of fibrin sealant," Acta Neurochir. (Suppl.) **43**, 193–197 (1968).
216. A.S. Genest, "Experimental use of intraluminal plastics in the treatment of carotid aneurysms," J. Neurosurg. **22**, 136–140 (1965).
217. J.F. Alksne, "Stereotactic thrombosis of intracranial aneurysms," N. Engl. J. Med. **284**, 171–174 (1971).
218. J.F. Alksne, A.G. Fingerhut, and R.W. Rand, "Magnetically controlled metallic thrombosis of intracranial aneurysms," Surgery **60**, 212–218 (1966).
219. W.J. German and S.P.W. Black, "Intra-aneurysmal hemodynamics—jet action," Circ. Res. **3**, 463–468 (1955).
220. E.S.K. Kwan, C.B. Heilman, W.A. Shucart, and R.P. Klucznik, "Enlargement of basilar artery aneurysms following balloon occlusion—water-hammer effect. Report of two cases," J. Neurosurg. **75**, 963–968 (1991).

221. W. Grand, "Preoperative blood pressure in the aneurysm patient," in *Clinical Management of Intracranial Aneurysms*, edited by L.N. Hopkins and D.M. Long (Raven, New York, 1982), pp. 29–38.
222. P.S. Slosberg, "Treatment of ruptured intracranial aneurysms by induced hypotension," Mount Sinai J. Med. N.Y. **40**, 82–90 (1973).
223. D.J. Valentino, V. Bhushan, R. Kiss, M. Harreld, R. Lufkin, F. Viñuela, and D. Gibson, "Virtual reality in radiology: innovative applications of PACS in neuroradiology," in *Medical Imaging 1994: Image Capture, Formatting, and Display*, edited by Y. Kim, Proc. SPIE **2164**, 393–401 (1994).
224. N.M. Oyesiku, A.R.T. Colohan, D.L. Barrow, and A. Reisner, "Cocaine-induced aneurysmal rupture: An emergent negative factor in the natural history of intracranial aneurysms?" Neurosurgery **32**, 518–526 (1993).
225. P. Gras, D. Martin, and M. Giroud, "Aneurysm rupture and cocaine addiction," Neurochirurgie **37**, 403–405 (1991).
226. R. Green, K.M. Kelly, T. Gabrielson, S.R. Levine, and C. Vandersant, "Multiple intracerebral hemorrhages after smoking crack cocaine," Stroke **21**, 957–962 (1990).

6.11 Problems

6.1. The qualitative effects of atherosclerosis or blockage of a vessel on hemodynamics were described in the text as it relates to the development of fusiform aneurysms. How can this be shown or explained with common, readily available equipment?

6.2. What are the primary requirements for an embolic agent?

6.3. What are the consequences of a partially embolized aneurysm?

6.4. What are potential problems of coils used in the endovascular treatment of aneurysms?

6.5. If a hypothetical drug were available to treat an aneurysm, what would most likely be its mechanism or target?

6.6. What are the most important aneurysm parameters dictating the type of therapy?

6.7. Abdominal aortic aneurysms (AAA) represent one form of fusiform aneurysm that can be extremely dangerous upon rupture. Why is this the case?

6.8. (A) Assuming R_i is the radius of the aneurysm neck, derive an expression for the neck diameter based on Laplace's law. (**B**) What is the primary assumption in stating R_i is the aneurysm neck?

6.9. Laplace's law for an elastic sphere holds under the condition $h/R \ll 1$. What would the circumferential stress be for an elastic sphere exhibiting $h \approx R$?

6.10. Derive Laplace's law based on Newton's third law.

6.11. Derive an expression for the elastic modulus of an aneurysm based on its structural appearance at angiography.

6.12. In the biomathematical treatment of the fusiform aneurysm, $\phi = 0°$ reveals a negative expression for the critical radius. What does this mean?

6.13. What is the influence of increased elastic modulus on the resonant frequency of the aneurysm?

6.14. Describe several scenarios for which rupture due to resonance might be possible.

6.15. What are the effects of thrombus on the hemodynamics within the aneurysm?

6.16. For a given elastic material, the plot of stress versus strain reveals a linear curve followed abruptly by a rapidly increasing curve. (A) What physical explanations exist for the inflection point of the curve? (B) How is it determined mathematically?

6.17. Suppose that an electrolytically detachable coil has been delivered into an aneurysm creating a hoop of radius R. As current is being administered to detach the coil, a magnetic field is generated by the current through the coil. What is the magnetic field at points a distance x along the axis of the circular coil?

6.18. Endovascular therapeutic techniques involve the physical transformation of energy. Describe the various stages of energy transfer observed in the following: electrically detachable coils, radio-frequency probe, laser, biocompatible adhesives, ultrasound, systemic hypotension, and intravascular stents.

6.19. How can one easily determine the flow rate through a vascular phantom using a water faucet?

6.20. What is the physical principle behind Laplace's law?

6.21. What are the type of waves produced by the intra-aneurysmal sounds or bruits?

6.22. Proper delivery of a balloon in the treatment of aneurysms involves inflation into the aneurysm cavity. What would happen if the balloon were prematurely inflated?

6.23. For a fusiform aneurysm, derive an approximation for the volume of thrombus.

6.24. Given a round aneurysm with an intra-aneurysmal pressure of 150 mm Hg and a radius of 2.5 mm, calculate the corresponding force, in newtons, acting on the aneurysm wall.

7
The Physics of Intracranial Arteriovenous Malformations

7.1 Introduction

In this chapter, the biophysical and hemodynamic interactions involved in the development, diagnosis, and treatment of intracranial arteriovenous malformations are discussed. The primary objectives of this chapter are to provide the reader with knowledge of (1) the clinical epidemiology or prevalence of intracranial arteriovenous malformations; (2) the various types and associated features of intracranial arteriovenous malformations; (3) the biophysical and physiological basis for the diagnosis and therapy of intracranial arteriovenous malformations; (4) the theoretical and experimental methods to investigate the pathophysiology of intracranial arteriovenous malformations; and (5) a review of techniques for the diagnosis and therapy of intracranial arteriovenous malformations.

In the normal human circulation, the blood vessels originate from the heart and consists of a branching arrangement of arteries of continually decreasing size until they feed into a capillary bed before exiting the bed through small veins which increase in size prior to returning to the heart. As detailed in Chap. 3, the capillary bed serves an important purpose in that its vascular resistance slows the flow of blood considerably to allow perfusion of oxygen and nutrients to surrounding tissue and removal of cellular waste. In one form of cerebrovascular disease, arteriovenous malformations (AVMs), the vessels comprising the capillary bed of the brain, become malformed during embryonic development and prohibit the opportunity for blood to properly perfuse into the surrounding tissue.

AVMs are congenital vascular lesions that occur as a result of capillary maldevelopment between the arterial and venous systems.[1] As is the case with aneurysms, AVMs may occur at any point within the human vasculature, but are commonest and pose a more substantial risk to the patient when located in the brain. The vessels comprising the AVM are weak and enlarged and serve as direct shunts for blood flow between the high-pressure arterial system and the low pressure venous system, corresponding to a large pressure gradient and small vascular resistance. The abnormal low-resistance, high-flow shunting of blood within the brain AVM without an intervening capillary bed causes the fragile dilated vessels in the nidus to become structurally abnormal and fatigued, to enlarge further, and to possibly rupture.

Approximately 0.14% of the United States population has an intracranial AVM.[2] Brain AVMs pose a significant risk and represent a major life threat, particularly to persons under the age of 50. AVMs tend to produce symptoms in those between 20 and 40 years of age, occurring in a young and productive age group in which hemorrhage can be severely incapacitating or fatal.[3] By the end of the fourth decade of life, approximately 80% of all AVMs have become symptomatic, and 20% remain silent clinically and are more commonly diagnosed incidentally. Hemorrhage is the most serious sequela of AVMs, accounting for 50% of their clinical presentation and approximately 25% present with epileptic seizures.[4] The remaining percentage present as a result of mass effect, neurological deficits, or headaches. The incidence of initial AVM hemorrhage is approximately 3% per year with the mortality rate from an initial hemorrhage ranging from 10% to 17% and a severe disability rate of 20% to 29%.[3] Once an AVM has bled, the risk of a second hemorrhage, known as a rebleed, increases from 3% to 6%. In addition, headaches, dizziness, mass effect, and neurological deficits may occur as a consequence of brain AVMs.

7.2 Natural History of Intracranial Arteriovenous Malformations

Preoperative evaluation and management of intracranial AVMs are based primarily on the natural history, diagnostic presentation and interpretation, and the clinical status of the patient.[5] In the previous chapter, a host of factors involving the natural history of aneurysms, i.e., origin and development, was described in detail. These factors were classified as either congenital or acquired, with each being hypothesized as to their possible role in the development of intracranial aneurysms. In contrast, AVMs are believed to be congenital since they arise primarily as a defect in the early embryonic stages of capillary development (between the third and seventh week of gestation). Although AVMs are linked to embryonic processes, they paradoxically tend to manifest themselves clinically in adulthood. However, in comparison to patients with aneurysms, AVMs become symptomatic and/or rupture in patients younger than those with aneurysms.

Experimental and clinical investigations of AVMs have advanced current clinical knowledge of their anatomy, physiology, histology, diagnosis, and therapy. Of particular importance is the advancing techniques and instrumentation in the treatment of AVMs. Since the majority of AVMs are symptomatic lesions,[1] an aggressive therapeutic approach should be implemented upon diagnosis. The underlying goal in the treatment of AVMs is to restrict blood flow through the AVM and redirect it through the normal brain circulation. Active treatment remains the option for the great majority (between 60% and 80%) of patients harboring an AVM. This can be accomplished at risk levels to the patient that are less than 50% of those AVMs not treated.[2] Methods of therapy and their underlying principles will be described later in this chapter.

7.3 Anatomy and Physiology of Intracranial Arteriovenous Malformations

Since intracranial AVMs evolve presumably as a result of a defect in the embryonic stages of vascular development, the anatomy and physiology of the lesion, particularly as it relates to their natural history, are critically important in assessing their growth and development. AVM anatomy and physiology also represent factors that influence their propensity to rupture. In fact, the anatomy or angioarchitecture and physiology or hemodynamics of AVMs have been studied with regard to such objectives and will now be described.

7.3.1 Anatomy of Intracranial AVMs

The angioarchitecture or structural arrangement of an intracranial AVM, depicted in Fig. 7.1, consists of three distinct vascular components: (1) nidus, (2) arterial feeders, and (3) draining veins.

Nidus. Nidus is a term that represents the tangled conglomerate of weakened capillary vessels and is the central unit or core of an AVM. These abnormal capillary vessels serve as passive conduits for blood flow from the arterial circulation directly to the venous circulation, bypassing their normal physiological function of brain tissue perfusion. The nidus vessels typically assume a plexiform or mesh arrangement, particularly for the smaller AVMs. In larger AVMs, an intranidal fistula or a direct connection between an artery (arterial feeder) and vein (draining vein) has been observed clinically. We would like to digress from our discussion on AVMs for a moment to focus on arteriovenous fistulae (AVFs).

An AVF, although it occurs with great frequency in larger AVMs, is also clinically observed as an isolated lesion. Although AVFs also occur anywhere within the human body, they can develop as a result of a traumatic episode involving a specific anatomic region where an artery and vein are in close proximity, such as a penetrating gunshot wound involving the femoral artery and femoral vein of the upper thigh.[6] Regardless of their natural history, the hemodynamic consequences of an AVF remain the same as AVMs in that a shunting of blood occurs between artery and vein. A direct con-

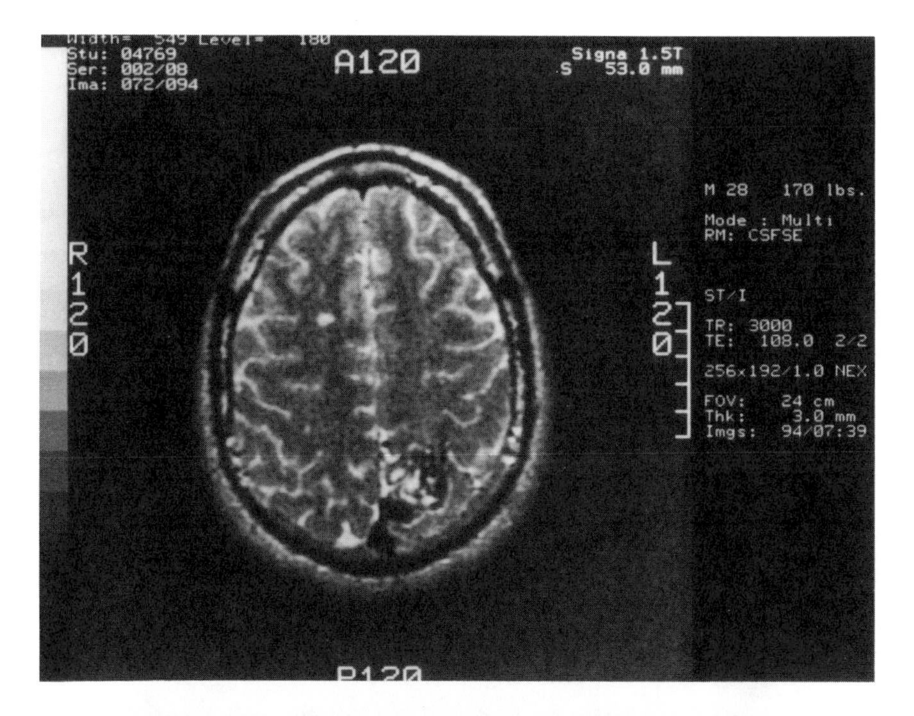

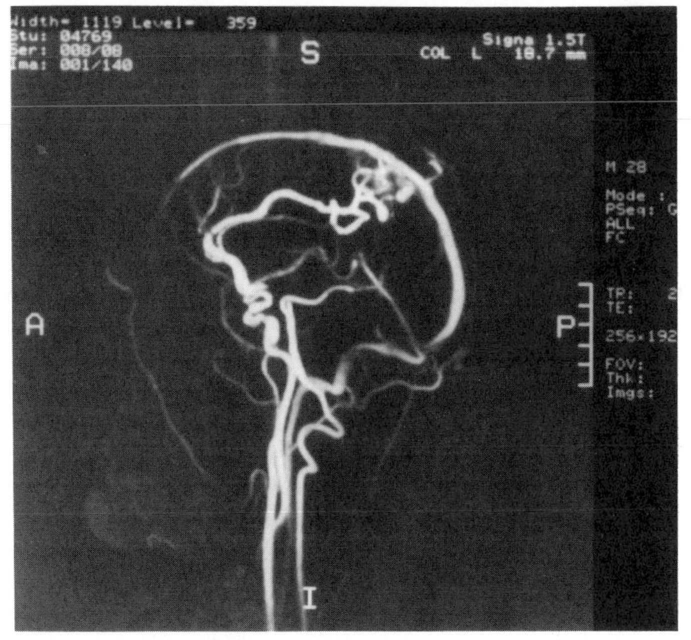

FIGURE 7.1. Schematic diagram of an intracranial arteriovenous malformation, depicting the structural and angioarchitectural components.

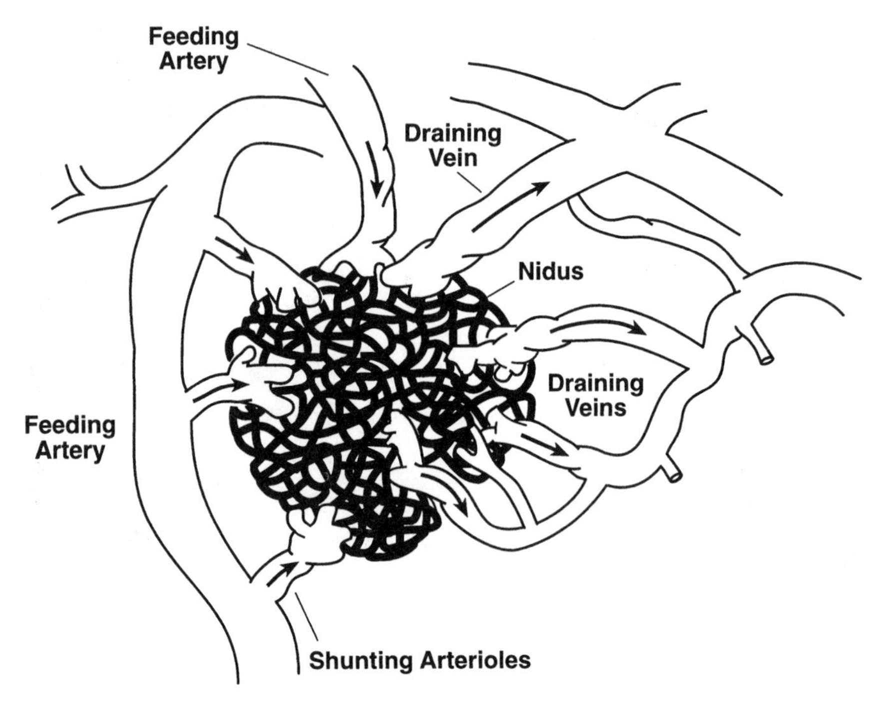

FIGURE 7.1 (*continued*)

nection between the arterial and venous systems establishes two circuits of flowing blood: (a) the normal circuit of high peripheral resistance and high arterial pressure, and (b) the fistula circuit of low peripheral resistance and low venous pressure, into which a volume of blood from the normal circulatory bed is forced continuously and inexorably through the fistula by the high arterial pressure of the normal circuit.[7] The clinical consequences of a fistula is a significant increase in blood returning to the heart ($\approx$4–5 times the original amount, depending on the diameter and size of the fistulous vessel), resulting in a dangerous overload of the heart and possible cardiac failure. For additional reading, the reader is urged to consult the work by Strandness,[8] Strandness and Sumner,[9] Binak et al.,[10] and Frank et al.[11]

Returning to our discussion on AVMs, the plexiform arrangement of nidus vessels can either occur as a compact nidus where the vessels are efficiently contained within a well-defined volumetric geometry or as a diffuse nidus in which the nidus vessels are distributed more diffusely from the AVM core. Pathological studies have shown that plexiform vessels in human AVMs may assume four distinct vessel types ranging in size or diameter from 0.15 to 1.0 mm.[12]

Arterial feeders. Arterial feeders are large arteries, usually branching from the circle of Willis, that serve as direct feeders or flow inlets into the nidus.

The number, size, and hemodynamics of arterial feeders are crucial in the diagnostic assessment, management, and therapy of AVMs and vary typically according to AVM size and location. Arterial feeders represent the safest of all vascular points within the AVM where pressure measurements can be made. A microcatheter for pressure measurements can be navigated through the major blood vessels of the body, into the cerebral circulation, and situated within the major arterial feeders.[13] The microcatheter can even reach the distal end of the arterial feeder, just at the periphery of the AVM nidus. Mean arterial feeder pressures obtained with a microcatheter range from 21 to 80 mm Hg with the larger pressures characteristic of the smaller feeders.[14] The nidus vessels themselves are too weak and small to accommodate even minor perturbations produced by the movement of a microcatheter and are thus inaccessible to any type of direct *in vivo* hemodynamic measurements.

Draining veins. Draining veins are large veins that serve as direct drainage or flow outlets from the nidus. The draining veins are the largest of the AVM components, easily identifiable at angiography, with the size or diameter of typical draining veins approximately 5.0 mm. As is the case with arterial feeders, a microcatheter could, in principle, be navigated through the venous system for pressure measurements at the draining veins of the AVM. However, draining veins, as is characteristic of the mechanical properties of venous wall, are thin-walled and could easily be traumatized with improper advancement of the microcatheter. Thus, operator experience is a critical factor in hemodynamic measurements with a microcatheter, regardless of whether the vessel is an arterial feeder or draining vein. In any event, mean intravascular draining vein pressures range from 5 to 23 mm Hg.[14]

The size of an AVM, denoted as the maximum diameter $D_{\max}$ of the nidus varies in the range 1–10 cm. Clinical descriptions of AVM size include small ($D_{\max} < 3$ cm), accounting for approximately 30% of the afflicted population; medium ($3\,\text{cm} \leq D_{\max} \leq 6\,\text{cm}$), accounting for 60%; and large ($D_{\max} > 6\,\text{cm}$), accounting for 10%.[15] Volume measurements, which are particularly useful in decisions regarding therapy, are approximated from the equation for the volume of an ellipsoid[16]:

$$V = \frac{4}{3}\pi R_a R_b R_c.$$

A factor of significance concerning AVM size is the clinical observation that smaller AVMs exhibit a higher propensity or likelihood to rupture than the larger ones. In smaller AVMs, this may be due to the impact of the hemodynamic effects of the rapid shunting of blood flow being less dissipated and more forcefully registered within the nidus. This issue will be discussed in more detail later in this chapter.

Possible growth of an AVM is characterized not only by vessel enlargement of the present nidus vessels but also by the recruitment of adjacent normal vessels of the brain. As the AVM becomes larger, the number of arterial feeders and draining veins increase and fistulous vessels are shown to appear. Although fistulae frequently occur in the human body without the malformed capillary bed, intranidal fistulae or fistulous vessels within the AVM nidus are commonly found in larger AVMs.

According to the literature, the nidus of a large AVM is believed to be compartmentalized either structurally[17] or functionally.[18,19] Structural compartmentalization assumes that groups of nidus vessels are morphologically independent from other vessels within the nidus in the form of separate compartments. This would imply that no recirculation or redistribution of hemodynamic forces occurs between compartments upon any perturbation of flow within the AVM nidus. Functional compartmentalization involves groups of nidus vessels that are connected anatomically but where blood mixing does not occur during transit from the arterial feeder to the draining vein due to a hemodynamic equilibrium between compartments.

7.3.2 Hemodynamics of Intracranial AVMs

Hemodynamics plays an instrumental role in all developmental and therapeutic aspects of AVMs.[20–24] Most importantly, hemodynamics are strongly believed to be a primary contributing factor in AVM rupture.[25] Due to the weak, fragile structure of the nidus vessels and the resolution limit of most imaging modalities, AVM hemodynamic assessment is restricted clinically to measurements at the arterial feeders and draining veins, leading one to only speculate about flow within the AVM nidus. A standard global measurement of AVM hemodynamics is the total blood flow through the AVM. The total blood flow is typically determined through catheter measurements of flow in the arterial feeders of vessels feeding blood into the AVM nidus. Since the volume of blood entering the AVM is equal to the volume exiting the AVM by the conservation of mass, total blood flow could also be obtained by catheter measurements of flow in the draining veins but pose more of a safety risk than flow measurements in the arterial feeders. In a human AVM, blood flows from the arterial feeders (AFs) (diameter 2–3 mm), to shunting arterioles (diameter 50–200 μm), through the nidus vessels (diameter $\approx 250\,\mu$m), to venous loops (diameter 50–200 μm), to venules or collecting veins (diameter 200–300 μm), and exits the major draining veins (DVs) (diameter 5.0 mm).[18] However, a more realistic description of intranidal hemodynamics is that flow from an AF enters the nidus through a vessel in the nidus that is positioned arbitrarily, not one that is necessarily connected to the AF at an opposite pole to where the DVs are. Blood flow[26] through an AVM ranges from 200 to 800 ml/min and increases according to nidus size. For localized hemodynamics within a particular vessel of an AVM such as an AF or DV, we can employ the same principles first introduced in Chap. 4.

As is the case for any blood vessel, proper characterization of blood flow within the nidus vessels of the AVM consists of a non-Newtonian fluid flowing in a pulsatile nature through a viscoelastic, tapered cylindrical vessel that requires complex mathematics and computationally intensive calculations. However, due to the small size of the vessels involved in the AVM, the hemodynamics of AVMs, as evidenced by previous experimental and theoretical studies, can be sufficiently approximated by the elementary principles and concepts presented by Poiseuille's formula[21,22]:

$$Q = \frac{\pi \Delta P R^4}{8 L \eta}, \tag{7.1}$$

where Q is the volumetric flow rate, ΔP is the pressure gradient, R is the inner radius of the vessel, L is the length of the vessel, and η is the blood viscosity ($\eta = 3.5$ cP). Equation (7.1) can be further simplified as

$$Q = \frac{\Delta P}{R_v}, \tag{7.2}$$

where R_v is the vascular resistance by the vascular bed given by

$$R_v = \frac{8 L \eta}{\pi R^4}. \tag{7.3}$$

Hemodynamics according to Poiseuille's law hold assuming that autoregulation does not occur. Another hemodynamic parameter of importance is the wall shear stress, accounting for the structural fatigue of the nidus vessel wall and contributing to AVM rupture. The wall shear stress τ in terms of the volumetric flow rate is given as

$$\tau = \frac{4 \eta Q}{\pi R^3}. \tag{7.4}$$

From the above relation, it can be seen that the more tortuous the nidus vessels are, the smaller the radius of curvature and the larger the wall shear stress.

7.3.2.1 Cerebrovascular Steal

The abnormal shunting of blood flow by brain AVMs rapidly removes or "steals" blood from the normal cerebral circulation and substantially reduces the volume of blood reaching the surrounding normal brain tissue. This phenomenon, which depends on the size of the AVM, is the most plausible explanation for the development of progressive neurological deficits[27] and could translate into additional neurological complications developed as a result of cerebral ischemia or stroke in neuronal territories adjacent to or even distant from an AVM. However, consensus among the neurosurgical community regarding steal as an established mechanism in the pathophysiology of AVMs does not exist. According to Diehl *et al.*[28] studies using a variety of cerebral blood flow measurement techniques have indicated normal blood flow in the tissue surrounding AVMs,[29] while others have demonstrated regions of decreased tissue perfusion in areas surrounding the AVM as well as at more distant sites and in the contralateral hemisphere.[30,31] However, in a large prospective study, Mast *et al.*[32] concluded that there was not sufficient evidence to assign steal as an operative pathophysiological mechanism in the vast majority of AVM patients.

A mathematical approximation of the reduced flow to adjacent regions of the brain as a result of an AVM commonly observed in cerebrovascular steal can be derived by assuming that the brain and AVM are two compartments connected in parallel.[33] According to the theoretical calculations by Lo, the total blood flow to the brain, F_{tot}, is related to the two components represented by the adjacent brain, F_b, and the AVM, F_{AVM}, according to

$$F_{\text{tot}} = F_b + F_{\text{AVM}}$$

with

$$F_b = \frac{\text{CPP}}{R_b}, \quad F_{\text{AVM}} = \frac{\text{CPP}}{R_{\text{AVM}}},$$

where CPP is cerebral perfusion pressure and R_b and R_{AVM} are the resistances of the adjacent brain region and the AVM, respectively. It thus follows that the blood flow to adjacent regions of the brain is given by

$$F_b = F_{\text{tot}} - F_{\text{AVM}} = F_{\text{tot}} - \frac{\text{CPP}}{R_{\text{AVM}}}$$

7.3.2.2 Autoregulatory Capacity

Autoregulation is the biological ability of a blood vessel to regulate flow in response to acute and chronic changes in systemic physiology and is exhibited by every normal artery in the human body. However, controversy exists as to whether AVM nidus vessels or normal blood vessels adjacent to the AVM possess the capability to autoregulate blood flow through the nidus. According to Nornes and Grip,[22] "AVM vessels are viewed as fixed vascular conduits; they do not autoregulate in response to changes in arterial blood pressure and do not respond to chemical stimuli such as arterial CO^2. This suggests that increases in arterial blood pressure would be transmitted directly to AVM vessels." However, in a recent study by Young *et al.*,[34] evidence was found to suggest that an AVM is capable of some, as yet undefinable, degree of autoregulation.

Autoregulatory vasoconstriction in vascular beds adjacent to the AVM has been observed and described previously with arterial pressures as low as 30 mm Hg.[35] Autoregulation can be described mathematically as a relation between the current vessel radius and the original vessel radius subjected to changes in transmural pressure,[36]

$$r = r_0 + mP_{\text{tr}},$$

where r and r_o are the current and initial radii of the nidus vessel, respectively, P_{tr} is the transmural pressure, and m is a proportionality constant representing the change in radius versus a corresponding change in transmural pressure.

7.4 Experimental Models of Intracranial AVMs

The importance of AVM hemodynamics and their role in the growth, rupture, diagnosis, and therapy of AVMs has prompted the development of novel approaches in the form of models to qualitatively and quantitatively investigate hemodynamic phenomena in AVMs. Due to the natural history and potentially devastating consequences, clinical investigations of AVM hemodynamics are limited only to observations at diagnosis and at all stages of therapeutic intervention. Thus, two alternative approaches employed in the study of AVM hemodynamics are biomathematical models and experimental animal models.

7.4.1 Biomathematical Models

The purpose and role of biomathematical models are instrumental in the understanding of AVM physiology under normal hemodynamic conditions and during various types and stages of therapy. Models are necessary to achieve reproducibility—an essential component of scientific experimentation. An overall drawback inherent to all theoretical modeling is the lack of biological traits and biovariability, as may be available in naturally occurring or constructed *in vivo* models. However, biomathematical modeling and simulations are useful as a means of providing (1) a systematic and effective way of assembling existing knowledge about a system; (2) identification of important parameters and determination of the overall system sensitivity to variation in each parameter; (3) calculation of quantitative values of variables that are difficult or impossible to measure; (4) a method to test hypotheses rapidly, efficiently, and inexpensively; (5) identification of specific elements or information gaps that must be further quantified, thus leading to the development of important experiments or quantitative measures; and (6) an effective model which can be utilized to predict the behavior of a real system.[37] Each one of these factors are relevant in the development of an AVM model.

Biomathematical models have been used previously to study the hemodynamics of AVMs and their risk of hemorrhage.[14,33,36,38–41] Biomathematical models represent a theoretical method of investigating AVM hemodynamics but currently provide limited information due to the simplicity of simulated anatomical and physiological characteristics in available models. Previous biomathematical AVM models have typically involved multicompartmental analysis of nidus vessels arranged in a parallel and independent fashion with one arterial feeder and one draining vein. Although an intracranial AVM with one arterial feeder and one draining vein is somewhat uncommon, it should be the first type of model to be considered due to its simplicity. However, clinical and pathological examination of AVMs have shown that they much more often are fed and drained by multiple arterial feeders and draining veins.[42] Also, the tightly interwoven microvessels contained within the nidus are typically interconnected with many branches, at least bifurcations and trifurcations, making them extremely dependent on each other and on the hemodynamics at the feeding and draining pedicles.

The AVM model employed by Lo and colleagues[33,38,39] consisted of three linked compartments representing arterial feeders, shunting arterioles, and the core vessels of the AVM with flow draining into the central venous drainage. They have simulated hemodynamics within small and large AVMs with results comparable to those observed clinically but neglected the appearance of draining veins. Hecht, Horton, and Kerber[40] expanded upon this concept with simulations in an AVM nidus composed of 1000 nidus vessel compartments. Ornstein *et al.*[36] introduced a more complex AVM model by considering the influence of inductance, conductance, and autoregulation. They employed an electrical circuit analog to develop a simulated model of an AVM. Their AVM model consisted of a feeding artery, draining vein, and a capillary bed with an encased fistula. The study modeled the hemodynamic effects of AVM occlusion simulating neurosurgical resection and embolotherapy. All of these previous models present with common underlying limitations: (1) single AF and either a single DV or neglect of venous drainage, (2) compartmentalized nidus vessels, (3) omission of a fistulous component, which is a common occurrence in large AVMs, and (4) representation of the nidus as a single resistance or series of resistances. Modeling flow within the nidus by a single resistance or an array of resistances is probably justified since (1) it is virtually impossible to acquire any quantitative intranidal hemodynamic measurements at angiography or magnetic resonance imaging (MRI) and (2) intranidal flow is visually displayed at angiography as a rapid traversal of contrast agent through the AVM without any reference to anatomy or geometry, due primarily to the limited resolution of current imaging systems.

7.4.1.1 An Electrical Network Model of Intracranial AVMs

The concept of electrical networks can serve a unique purpose in the hemodynamic modeling of AVMs. As described in Chap. 4, fluid dynamics and, in particular, hemodynamics, can be represented with electrical analogs where fluid flow is represented by current, pressure gradient by voltage, and the resistance, in essence, remains the same. This approach was uniquely extended to the characterization of nidus vessels, which are not routinely visualized by current imaging technology but are understood primarily from post-mortem and histopathological analysis. Thus, an electrical network was developed in a form of a circuit to simulate the human circulation equipped with an AVM.[41] The computer-based electrical network model of a brain AVM based on realistic gross morphological, clinical, histopathological, angiographic and biophysical observations has been described and validated in an attempt to establish a tool capable of qualitative and quantitative elucidation of complex hemodynamics through an AVM and assess its risk of rupture at therapy.

The biomathematical AVM model described above was constructed to simulate closely the clinical features and anatomic landmarks typically seen in intracranial AVMs. The AVM network, nestled within a network representing the head and neck circulation, consists of four AFs, two DVs, and a nidal angioarchitecture with a randomly distributed array of 28 interconnected plexiform and fistulous components, as shown in Fig. 7.2. The fistulous component consisted of a direct connection between AF2 and DV1 with interconnecting plexiform vessels. Two AFs were considered major while the other two were minor.

In the circulatory system depicted in this model, blood flow is propagated by the heart under a systemic arterial blood pressure, E_{SP}, represented by an electromotive force and continues through the aortic arch to the first arterial bifurcation consisting of the common carotid artery (CCA) and the subclavian artery (SCA). Flow continues through the SCA to the vertebral artery (VA) followed by the posterior cerebral artery (PCA), which contributes a major AF (AF1). The CCA branches into the external carotid artery (ECA) and internal carotid artery (ICA). The ECA circulation is represented by a vascular network through the face, scalp, and skull and is shunted by a transdural minor AF (AF4) to the adjacent (intracranial) AVM vascular network. The ICA further branches as a trifurcation into the normal cerebrovasculature, the anterior cerebral artery (ACA), and the middle cerebral artery (MCA). The ACA contributes a minor AF (AF3) while the MCA is a major AF (AF2). The normal brain and AVM circulatory networks drain into the dural venous sinuses, the jugular veins, and the superior vena cava.

The vascular parameters employed in the AVM model are summarized in Table 7.1. In the network, pressures at major points within the circulatory network were assigned according to the following values, representing the arithmetic mean of common clinically observed values: mean systemic pressure 74 mm Hg; mean AF1 and AF2 pressures 47 mm Hg; mean AF3 and AF4 pressures 50 mm Hg; mean DV1 and DV2 pressures 17 mm Hg; mean central venous pressure 5 mm Hg. The mean pressure at AF3 and AF4 was defined to be slightly higher than that of AF1 and AF2 due to their much smaller size.

7.4.1.2.1 Electrical Network Analysis.

Solution of the AVM model depicted in Fig. 7.2 is obtained through electrical network analysis. Network analysis has been applied successfully to

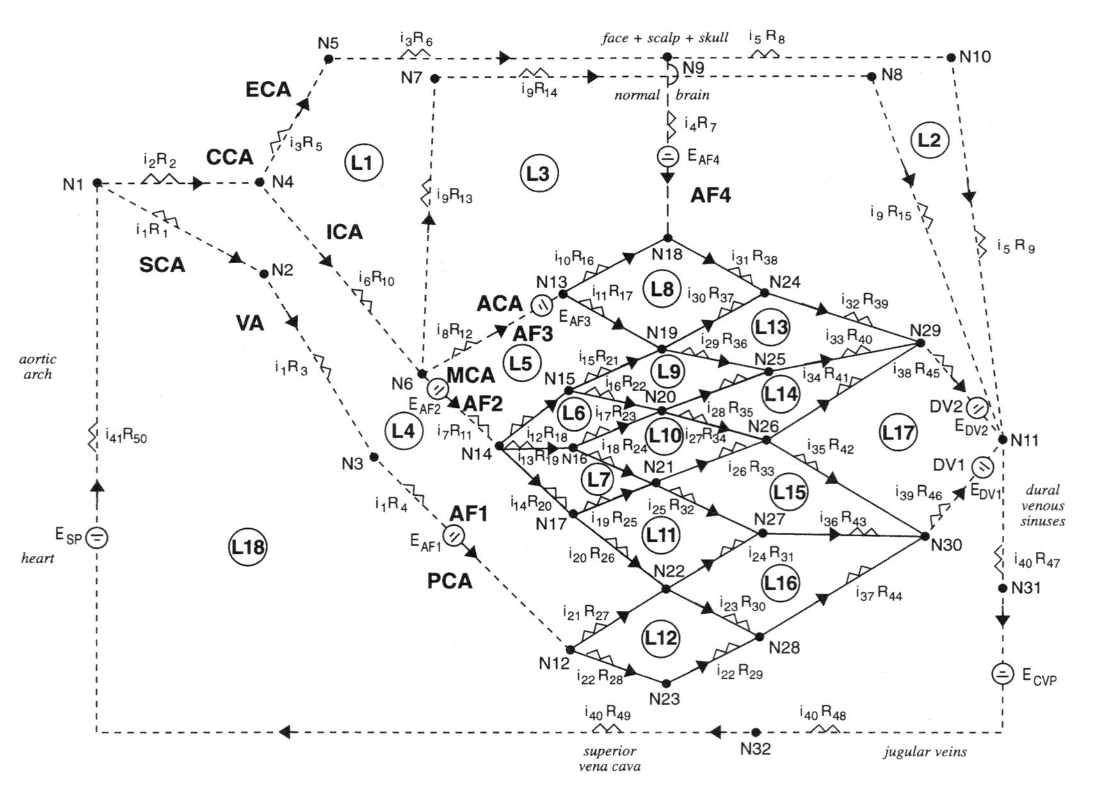

FIGURE 7.2. Schematic diagram of the electrical network describing the biomathematical AVM hemodynamic model. CCA represents common carotid artery; ECA, external carotid artery; ICA, internal carotid artery; SCA, subclavian artery; VA, vertebral artery; PCA, posterior cerebral artery; ACA, anterior cerebral artery; MCA, middle cerebral artery; E, electromotive force; AF, arterial feeder; DV, draining vein; N, node; L, loop. (Reprinted, with permission, from G.J. Hademenos, T.F. Massoud, and F. Viñuela, A biomathematical model of intracranial arteriovenous malformations based on electrical network analysis: Theory and hemodynamics. *Neurosurgery* **38**, 1005–1015, 1996.)

TABLE 7.1. Geometric and structural parameters for the vasculature represented in the biomathematical AVM model.

Vessel[a]	R^b (cm)	L^c (cm)	$R_v{}^d$ (dyn s/cm^5)
	Cardiovasculature		
N32–E_{SP} (Superior vena cava)	0.750	10.0	3.2
E_{SP}–N1 (Aortic arch)	1.000	10.0	1.0
N1–N2 (Subclavian artery)	0.350	10.0	67.9
	Head and neck vasculature		
Neck and extracranial circulation			
N1–N4 (Common carotid artery)	0.350	10.0	67.9
N4–N5 (External carotid artery)	0.200	10.0	637.5
N5–N9	CP bed	CP bed	1 000 000.0
N9–N10	CP bed	CP bed	1 000 000.0
N10–N11	0.125	10.0	4 177.9
N31–N32 (Jugular veins)	0.400	20.0	79.7
Intracranial circulation			
N4–N6 (Internal carotid artery)	0.250	20.0	522.0
N2–N3 (Vertebral artery)	0.150	25.0	5 037.0
N6–N7	0.100	10.0	10 200.0
N7–N8	CP bed	CP bed	1 000 000.0
N8–N11	0.125	10.0	4 177.9
N11–N31 (Dural venous sinuses)	0.250	10.0	261.0
	AVM vasculature		
Major arterial feeders			
AF1: N3–N12 (Posterior cerebral artery)	0.125	5.2	2 210.0
AF2: N6–N14 (Middle cerebral artery)	0.150	3.7	745.5
Minor arterial feeders			
AF3: N6–N13 (Anterior cerebral artery)	0.025	3.7	15 725 000.0
AF4: N9–N18 (Transdural feeding artery)	0.0125	3.0	12 750 000.0
Nidus vessels			
Plexiform	0.050	5.0	81 600.0
Fistulous	0.100	4.0	4 080.0
Draining veins			
DV1: N29–N11	0.250	5.0	130.5
DV2: N30–N11	0.250	5.0	130.5

[a] E_{SP}, electromotive force representing systemic pressure, CP, capillary, AF, arterial feeder; DV, draining vein; N, node

[b] R is the vessel radius.

[c] L is the vessel length.

[d] R_v is the vascular resistance.

the study of hemodynamics of systemic and pulmonary microcirculation in capillary beds.[43–48] In network analysis, vessels of various radii and lengths are randomly distributed in a dependent manner to resemble a highly disordered frame or network through which fluid will flow. In analogies found in electricity, the circulatory network can be represented by a complex electrical circuit of connected wires with variable resistance through which the current or flow, powered by an electric power source or pressure gradient, will traverse. Each wire or vessel connection represents a node or a location at which flow converges and diverges. With respect to the AVM, the node resembles the start or end of a vascular branch, e.g., bifurcation or trifurcation, within the vascular bed.

The flow proceeds from left (arterial feeders) to right (draining veins) and was calculated according to the following two rules[49]: (1) the algebraic sum of the currents at any node must be zero, i.e., flow into a node is equal to flow out of the node, and (2) the algebraic sum of the changes in potential (pressure gradient) encountered in a complete traversal of the circuit must be zero. More specifically, within a current loop, (A) if a resistor is traversed in the direction of the current, the change in pressure is $-QR_v$, and in the opposite direction it is $+QR_v$; and (B) if a seat of pressure (electromotive force) is traversed in the direction of the pressure, the change in $+QR_v$ is $+\Delta P$, and in the opposite direction it is $-\Delta P$.[49] The results of rule (1) (nodal equations) and rule (2) (loop equations) on the circuit comprising the AVM hemodynamic model yields 41 different equations corresponding to the 41 values of volumetric flow rate. These equations yield a system of linear equations with the number of unknowns equal to the number of vessels:

$$\Delta P = QR_v.$$

This can be expanded in matrix form as

$$\begin{bmatrix} \Delta P_1 \\ \Delta P_2 \\ \Delta P_3 \\ \vdots \\ \Delta P_{41} \end{bmatrix} = \begin{bmatrix} Q_1 \\ Q_2 \\ Q_3 \\ \vdots \\ Q_{41} \end{bmatrix} \cdot \begin{bmatrix} R_{1,1} & R_{1,2} & R_{1,3} & \cdots & R_{1,41} \\ R_{2,1} & R_{2,2} & R_{2,3} & \cdots & R_{2,41} \\ R_{3,1} & R_{3,2} & R_{3,3} & \cdots & R_{3,41} \\ \vdots & \vdots & \vdots & \ddots & \\ R_{41,1} & R_{41,2} & R_{41,3} & & R_{41,41} \end{bmatrix}.$$

The flow can then be solved by matrix inversion of the above relation:

$$Q = R_v^{-1} \Delta P$$

Once the volumetric flow rate Q is determined for each simulation, it then becomes possible to calculate other hemodynamic parameters such as intravascular pressure gradient $(\Delta P)_{\text{NV}}$ and biomechanical stress S. Using the resistance for each nidus vessel, the intravascular pressure gradient is quantitated according to

$$(\Delta P)_{\text{NV}} = (Q)_{\text{NV}}(R_v)_{\text{NV}},$$

where NV refers to the particular nidus vessel. From the flow rate, it is possible to calculate other hemodynamic parameters on a vessel-by-vessel basis for the AVM network including the flow velocity, intravascular pressure gradient, and wall shear stress using the expressions given in Chap. 4. In addition, the intravascular pressure gradient can be used to calculate the biomechanical stress of the nidus vessel from the relation

$$S = \frac{\Delta P R}{h},$$

where R is the radius of the vessel and h is the vessel wall thickness. More advanced calculations can be made concerning AVM hemodynamics with the inclusion of inertial and conductance effects. The AVM hemodynamic simulations, based on the elementary relationship given by Ohm's law, assumes a linear relationship between flow (current) and pressure gradient (voltage).

Initial simulations employing the vascular parameters listed in Table 7.1 revealed a total volumetric flow through the AVM of 814 ml/min and increased flow rate through the fistulous component. With regard to AVM hemodynamics, particularly in a nidus containing a fistula, one would expect a region of high flow within the nidus and regions of lower flow through the plexiform vessels comprising the majority of the nidus. The intranidal flow rate varied from 5.5 to 57.0 ml/min with an average of 31.3 ml/min for the plexiform vessels and from 595.1 to 640.1 ml/min with an average of 617.6 ml/min for the fistulous components.

The advantages presented by the electric network model include (1) accurate anatomical and geometrical representation of a nidus with both plexiform and fistulous components that are interconnected and of sizes typically found at histopathology; (2) the AVM is fed by multiple arterial feeders (two major feeders and two minor feeders, via the circle of Willis and the external carotid system) and drained by multiple veins; (3) the AVM model allows the investigation of hemodynamics under normal conditions and therefore may also allow the study of those changes occurring as a result of therapeutic interventions; (4) the AVM model can be amended easily to simulate the clinical presentation of any AVM by adjusting the number, size, length, location, and intravascular pressure of arterial feeders and draining veins; and (5) the AVM model reveals not only hemodynamic values within any feeding pedicle or nidus vessel but provides one with information regarding intranidal regions or areas of abnormal hemodynamics.

Theoretical Risk of AVM Hemorrhage. The most critical issue with regard to any perturbation exerted on the AVM nidus as a result of interventional therapy is the risk of AVM rupture and corresponding increases related to these perturbations. The risk of AVM rupture or hemorrhage is extremely difficult to quantify clinically and is expressed typically in relative probabilities based on a neurosurgeon's experience given similar types of AVMs. However, it is possible to mathematically derive an expression for the theoretical determination of risk of AVM rupture that can readily be calculated to each nidus vessel contained within the nidus following each simulation.

The highly tortuous, structurally weak intranidal vessels coupled with the continual impingement of large hemodynamic forces make the AVM highly susceptible to hemorrhage. The precise location or region of rupture is extremely difficult to observe angiographically and to detect histologically and remains a source of speculation in the assessment of AVMs. It is commonly believed that, based on the biomechanical properties of the intranidal vessels, rupture occurs when the cumulative hemodynamic stresses of the vessel wall exceed the elastic modulus.

In static equilibrium, the distribution of forces acting on the cylindrical vessel can be explained by Laplace's law. Laplace's law, in effect, equates a radial force P produced by the transmural blood pressure over the cross-sectional area of the lumen that distends it to a circumferential force T that compensates for the distension. In mathematical form, Laplace's law for a cylinder, as stated in Chap. 2, is

$$T = PR, \tag{7.5}$$

where R is the radius of curvature. The stress within the vessel wall can be determined by

$$S = \frac{PR}{h}, \tag{7.6}$$

where h is the wall thickness. Equation (7.6) is only valid, however, for thin-walled vessels, i.e., $h \ll R$. The integral factors which influence the wall stress can be shown by taking the differential of Eq. (7.6):

$$dS = d\left(\frac{PR}{h}\right) = \frac{R}{h}dP + \frac{P}{h}dR - \frac{PR}{h^2}dh. \tag{7.7}$$

The circumferential wall stress, given in Eq. (7.6), can also be expressed as

$$S = \varepsilon E, \tag{7.8}$$

where ε is the circumferential strain and E is the elastic modulus of the vessel under physiological conditions. The circumferential strain can be expressed as the ratio $\Delta R/R$, where ΔR is the change in radial length between the relaxed and strained states and R is the radial length in the unstrained state. Assuming that changes in the radial length are infinitesimal, Eq. (7.8) can be expressed in differential form as

$$dS = \frac{dR}{R}E. \tag{7.9}$$

Equating Eqs. (7.7) and (7.9),

$$\frac{R}{h}dP + \frac{P}{h}dR - \frac{PR}{h^2}dh = \frac{dR}{R}E. \tag{7.10}$$

The condition of vessel rupture or blowout can be derived by determining the differential relation between the radius and pressure, dR/dP. Dividing both sides of Eq. (7.10) by dP and solving for dR/dP,

$$\frac{dR}{dP} = \frac{\dfrac{R}{h} - \dfrac{PR}{h^2}\dfrac{dh}{dP}}{\dfrac{E}{R} - \dfrac{P}{h}}. \tag{7.11}$$

Expressing Eq. (7.11) in terms of volume can be accomplished by

$$\frac{dV}{dP} = \frac{dV}{dR}\frac{dR}{dP}, \tag{7.12}$$

where dV/dP is referred to as volume distensibility and V is the volume of a cylinder ($\pi R^2 L$). Thus

$$\frac{dV}{dP} = 2\pi RL\,\frac{dR}{dP}$$

or

$$\frac{dV}{dP} = 2\pi RL\,\frac{\dfrac{R}{h} - \dfrac{PR}{h^2}\dfrac{dh}{dP}}{\dfrac{E}{R} - \dfrac{P}{h}}. \tag{7.13}$$

Assuming that E is constant, the rate of volume expansion will continually increase with increasing pressure to the state where

$$\frac{E}{R} = \frac{P}{h}$$

Solving for R yields the critical radius R_c,

$$R_c = \frac{Eh}{P}. \tag{7.14}$$

Equation (7.14) describes the critical radius of the blood vessel. Any increase or decrease in the state variables that would upset this equality could possibly induce rupture. Evaluation of the risk of AVM rupture is based on the functional distribution of the critical radius with respect to the theoretical blood pressure extremes encountered by the nidus and is given by

$$\text{Risk of AVM rupture} = \frac{\displaystyle\int_{P_{\min}}^{P_{\exp}} \frac{Eh}{P}\,dP}{\displaystyle\int_{P_{\min}}^{P_{\max}} \frac{Eh}{P}\,dP}, \tag{7.15}$$

where $P_{\min}$ and $P_{\max}$ are the central venous pressure (CVP) and the "maximum intranidal pressure," respectively, and $P_{\exp}$ is the pressure of the nidus vessel determined at simulation.

We must now assign limits to the integral in the expression of risk of rupture according to the biophysical interactions exerted on the AVM nidus within extreme physiological conditions. In other words, we would like to incorporate the minimum and maximum values of pressure possibly attainable in a human AVM nidus. The lowest attainable pressure experienced by an AVM would be equal to the mean central venous pressure or $P_{min} = 6.6 \times 10^3$ dyn/cm^2 (equivalent to a CVP of 5 mm Hg). The upper limit of arterial pressure experienced by the nidus microvessels before rupture is likely to occur during considerable systemic hypertension (that is, blood pressure that is then transmitted to the arterial feeders and the nidus). It has been observed at least that systemic hypertension and abnormal levels of blood pressure up to a mean value of 118 mm Hg do not precipitate AVM hemorrhage.[50] The influence of higher levels of systemic hypertension on the propensity of AVMs to rupture is unknown. Therefore, one must assume that the normally low-pressure arterial feeders may reach a maximum value of 74 mm Hg during mean systemic hypertensive levels of 118 mm Hg (derived by assuming a linear relationship between these two parameters[51]). The value of 74 mm Hg (equivalent to 9.8×10^4 dyn/cm^2) is therefore chosen (somewhat conservatively) as the upper limit of blood pressure (P_{max}) possibly encountered by nidus vessels before rupture. It is noted that maximal arterial feeder pressures obtained by Young *et al.*[51] upon systemic hypertensive challenges reached values close to 74 mm Hg.

Due to the limited imaging resolution of most modalities, it is impossible to quantitatively determine the elastic modulus E and wall thickness h of the nidus vessels from *in vivo* imaging techniques. In light of this, they can be assumed constant and factored from the equation for risk of rupture. Evaluation of Eq. (7.15) yields the following expression for risk of AVM nidus rupture:

$$\text{Risk of AVM rupture} = \frac{\ln\left(\dfrac{P_{exp}}{P_{min}}\right)}{\ln\left(\dfrac{P_{max}}{P_{min}}\right)} \times 100\%. \tag{7.16}$$

The expression given in Eq. (7.16) represents the normalized probability or risk of rupture and is multiplied by 100% to present the results as a percentage of risk of rupture. The denominator or normalization constant is the integrated distribution of critical radii for the maximum possible transnidal pressure gradient. It can be seen that, on a qualitative basis, as the intravascular pressure of the nidus vessels reaches that of the "maximum intranidal pressure," the risk of rupture approaches 100%, implying certain rupture. Conversely, for intravascular pressures closer to that of central venous pressure, the risk of rupture decreases accordingly. Figure 7.3 shows the influence of intranidal vessel pressure on the risk of rupture. Risk of rupture is lowest at values closest to those of central venous pressure and increases in a

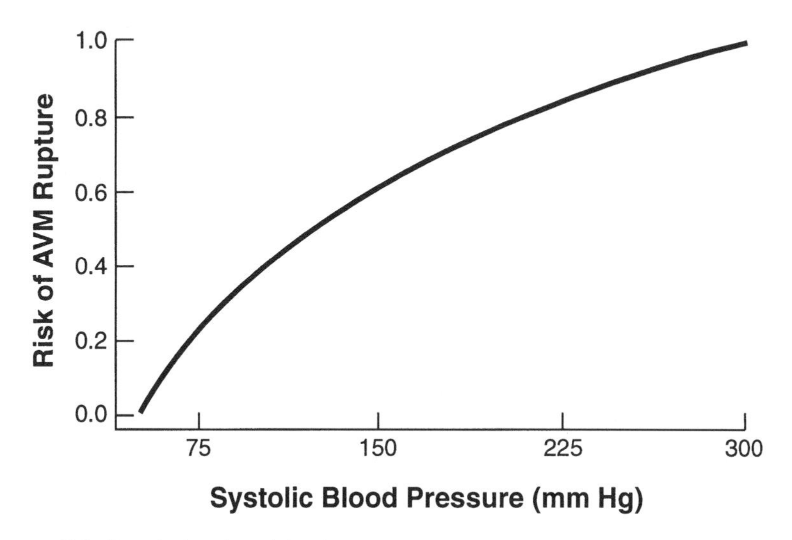

FIGURE 7.3. Graph showing risk of rupture versus intravascular pressure gradient for the nidus vessels. (Reproduced, with permission, from *Stroke*, **27**, G.J. Hademenos and T.F. Massoud, Risk of intractanial arteriovenous malformation rupture due to venous drainage impairment: A theoretical analysis, pp. 1072–1083. © 1996 American Heart Association.)

logarithmic fashion to a maximum value at pressures equal to or greater than the maximum intranidal pressure.

7.4.1.2.2 Applications of an Electrical Network AVM Model

Biomathematical models are as accurate as their inherent physical and mathematical complexity but provide the unique advantage of investigating the influence of biophysical and hemodynamic factors on clinically relevant issues involving physiology of the AVM in its normal state, at stages during and after therapeutic procedures, and subsequent abnormal conditions predisposing the AVM to rupture. Many examples of applications for the electrical network model include the study of (1) basic AVM hemodynamics; (2) basic pathophysiology; (3) adaptation to *in vivo* animal models and human AVMs; (4) angiographic observations; and (5) assessment of therapeutic procedures and strategies.

Example 1: Basic hemodynamics. One advantage of biomathematical models is the ability to theoretically construct an AVM to represent the structural or angioarchitectural characteristics of a unique or specific AVM based on preexisting knowledge from clinical, angiographic, histological, and biophysical analysis. The electrical network model described in the previous section was developed to simulate the hemodynamic characteristics of a high-flow–low-resistance medium to a large AVM with an intranidal fistula.

However, in reality, this represents only a fraction of AVM patient cases observed clinically. The question thus arises, "How, if possible, can a biomathematical model be adapted to represent a particular AVM seen in any given patient?" The various hemodynamic and biophysical parameters unique to an AVM, including the radii of intranidal vessels (plexiform and fistulous), systemic pressure, pressures at the feeding arteries and draining veins, elastic modulus, and wall thickness vary considerably within an AVM and among a given subset of AVMs.

Given the electrical network model (or any model for that matter), one must subject the model to ranges of typically observed values for each of the hemodynamic and biophysical parameters to monitor the qualitative and quantitative behavior of the AVM.[52] For the electrical network model, the criteria established to evaluate the behavior of the AVM as a result of variations of these parameters were twofold: (1) volumetric blood flow rate <900 ml/min and (2) a risk of rupture less than 100%. The result of such a study was that an infinite number of possible models exist, i.e., there is no single model that adequately represents all AVMs. Figure 7.4 depicts the flow chart describing the process of evaluating the AVM models and results for the ranges of systemic pressure, arterial feeder pressure, and draining vein pressure values for clinically acceptable AVM models according to the two criteria. Thus, by changing the above described hemodynamic and biophysical parameters implemented in the model within clinically observed ranges, this resulted in the creation of a large number of realistic models with varying hemodynamic features (all showing <900 ml/min and risk of AVM rupture <100%).

Example 2: Basic pathophysiology. Increased resistance in the venous drainage of cerebral AVMs may contribute to their increased risk of hemorrhage.[53–56] Venous drainage impairment may result from naturally occurring stenoses or occlusions, if draining veins undergo occlusion before feeding arteries during surgical removal, or following surgery in the presence of "occlusive hyperemia."[57,58] Venous drainage impairment is simulated in the model by substantially increasing the vascular resistance of the impaired draining vein, thereby restricting flow and obstructing the draining vein in a corresponding manner.[14] For example, let us consider the hemodynamic simulations through the AVM with both draining veins patent and with the progressive occlusion of DV1 by 25%, 50%, 75%, and 100% with DV2 fully patent. Each stage of occlusion was represented by its calculated value of resistance with the exception of 100%. Total occlusion of a vessel corresponded to an infinite resistance and was represented in the calculations by an extremely large value of resistance. As the draining veins are occluded, a resultant pressure buildup and transfer of pressure to nidus regions opposite the draining veins will occur. Given this, the questions that need addressing are: "By how much have the biomechanical stresses of the nidus vessels increased as a result of this pressure redistribution?" and "Is this sufficient to induce nidus rupture?"

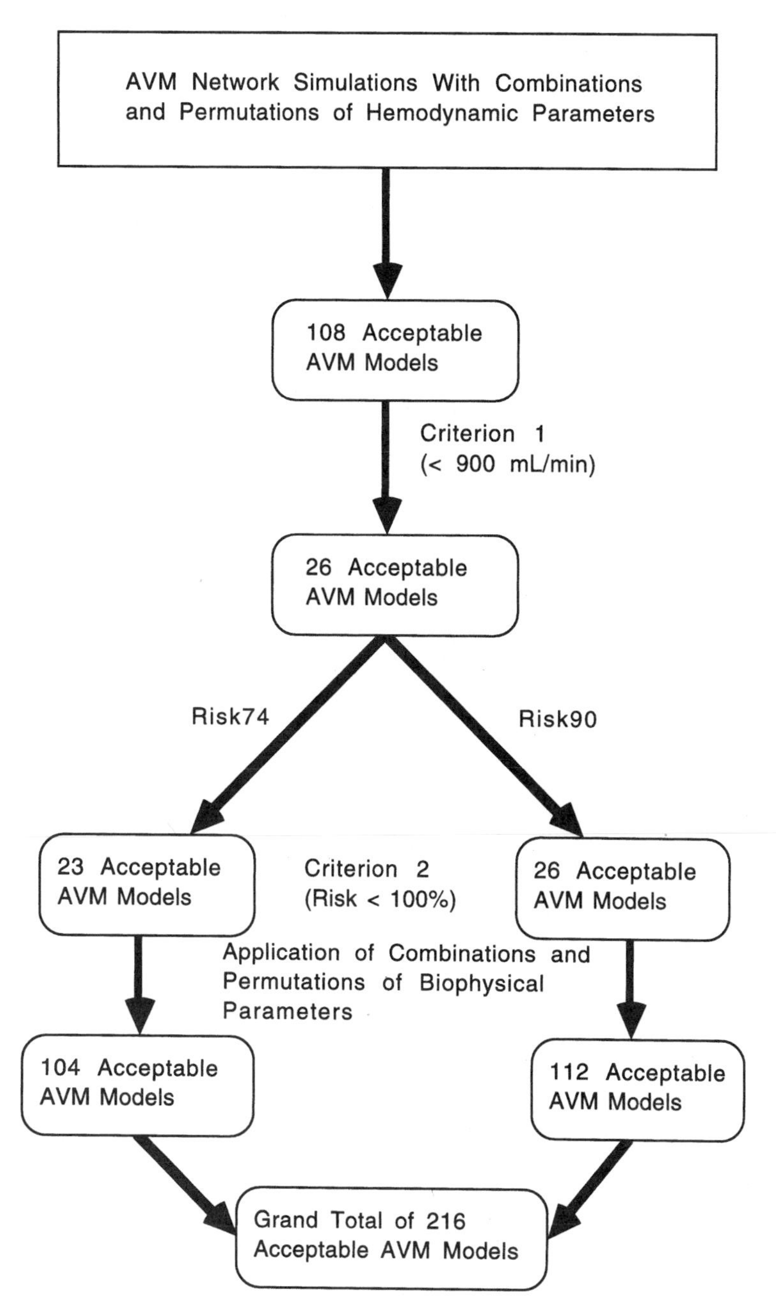

FIGURE 7.4. Left panel: Flow chart depicting the sequence of steps in the analysis and evaluation of the AVM electrical network simulations following implementation of criteria 1 and 2. Right panel: Histograms showing the risk of nidus rupture and volumetric flow rate values with respect to the minimum and maximum values of (A) mean systemic blood pressure, (B) mean arterial feeder pressure, and (C) mean draining vein pressure.

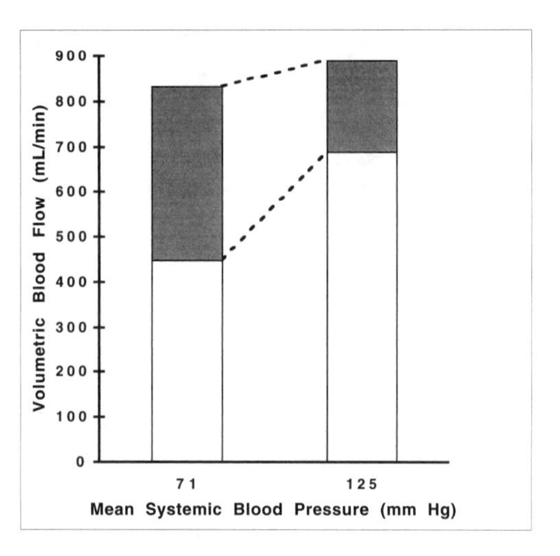

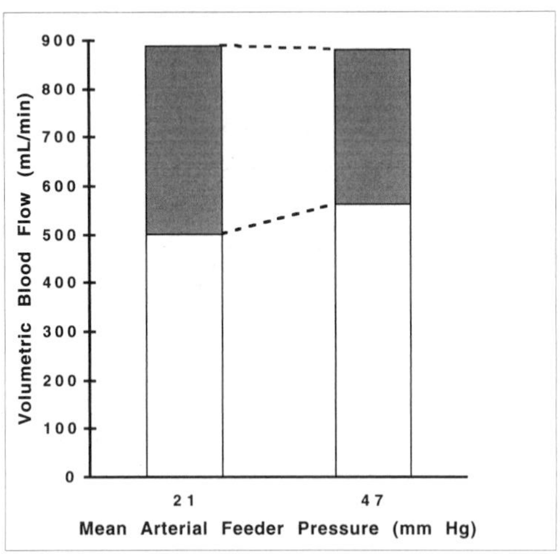

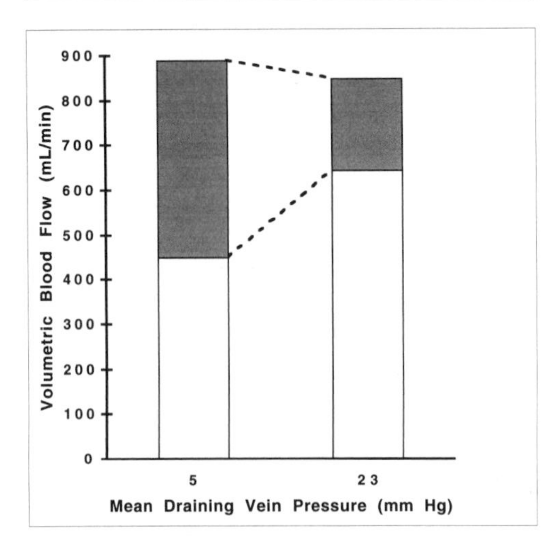

FIGURE 7.4 (*continued*)

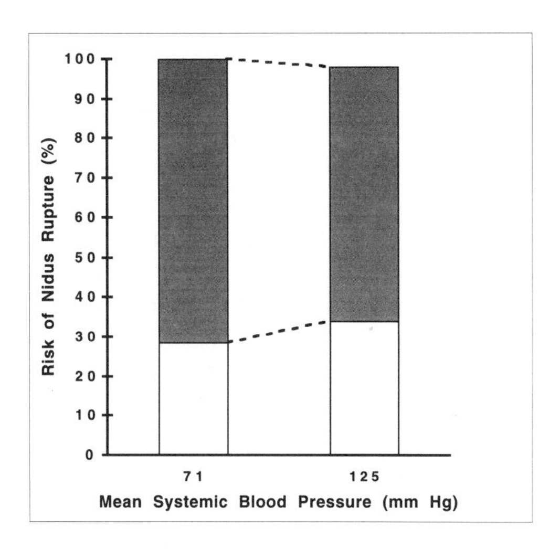

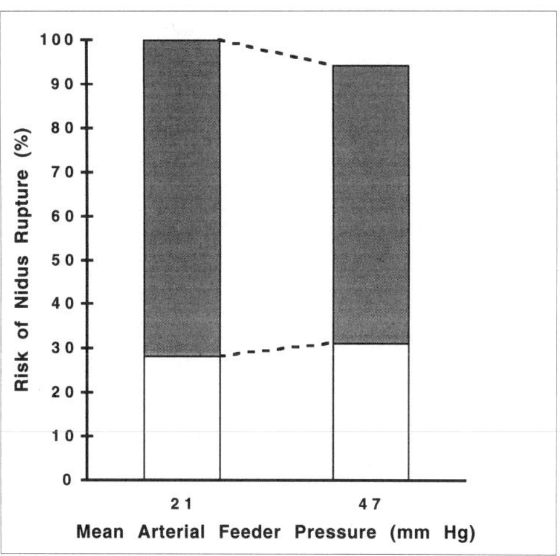

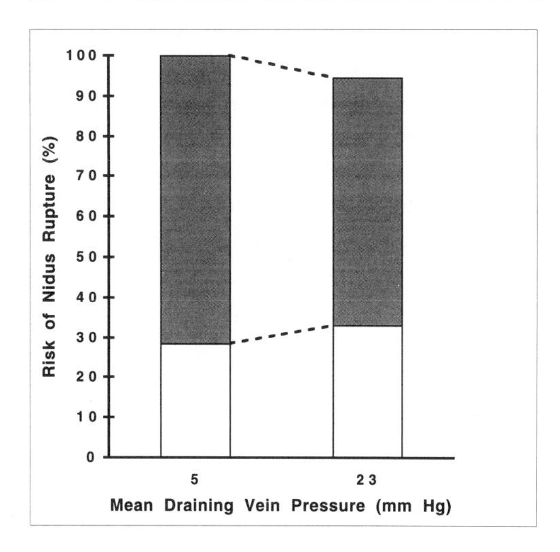

FIGURE 7.4 (*continued*)

The hemodynamic results from the AVM simulations presented in Fig. 7.5 show the individual values of intravascular pressure gradient, biomechanical stress, and risk of rupture within each nidus vessel mapped onto the AVM model network occurring as a result of the systematic occlusion of DV1 with DV2 patent displayed according to row. In the four simulations represented in Fig. 7.5 by the left-hand column, DV2 was patent and DV1 was occluded by 25% in simulation 2, 50% in simulation 3, 75% in simulation 4, and 100% in simulation 5. As one draining vein becomes occluded, the nidus vessels comprising the opposite side of the nidus compensate with increasing hemodynamic values. As DV1 becomes occluded, intravascular pressure in the upper portion of the nidus increases in response. In particular, notice the changes in biophysical and hemodynamic parameters of nidus vessels 34 and 35 as DV1 becomes occluded. Both nidus vessels assume the majority of the hemodynamic load and corresponding shift in intravascular pressure in response to the occlusion of the DV and, as can be seen from the nidus diagram for simulation 5, rupture occurs at nidus vessel 34.

Example 3: Adaptation of the electrical network model to in vivo experimental AVM models and human AVMs. Animal models provide a much more realistic representation of human AVMs and an accurate means of experimental *in vivo* investigation of hemodynamics and accompanying pathophysiological mechanisms before and following treatment techniques. *In vivo* AVM models have been created in rats,[59,60] cats,[61–63] swine,[64–68] and monkeys.[69] An important application of the electrical network model is adaptation to *in vivo* experimental AVM models and eventually human AVMs prompting one to consider the question, "How can the model be applied to simulate accurately AVM hemodynamics on a patient-by-patient basis?" In order to do so, one must improve upon the current two dimensional model in terms of geometry and complexity of the AVM nidus.

A human AVM typically consists of thousands of intertwined and branching vessels contained within an irregularly shaped nidus. Monte Carlo techniques or other similar computational techniques that employ random number generators to represent physical interactions or phenomena can be employed, not only to accommodate these constraints, but also to generate a more realistic, more complex AVM model using anatomical and physiological data, maintaining the three-dimensional (3D) spatial arrangement of nidus vessels, as shown in Fig. 7.6. The development of the more complex 3D AVM model could proceed in a manner described in Fig. 7.7 according to the following scheme.

1. Using a Monte Carlo program, the coordinates of a hypothetical brain AVM are mapped onto a 3D spatial plane and form the basis as a template for the nidus geometry and morphology of the AVM model.
2. At points spaced at predefined angular intervals from one another along the perimeter of the morphological geometry of the template, the Monte Carlo program randomly generates nidus vessels within the 3D tem-

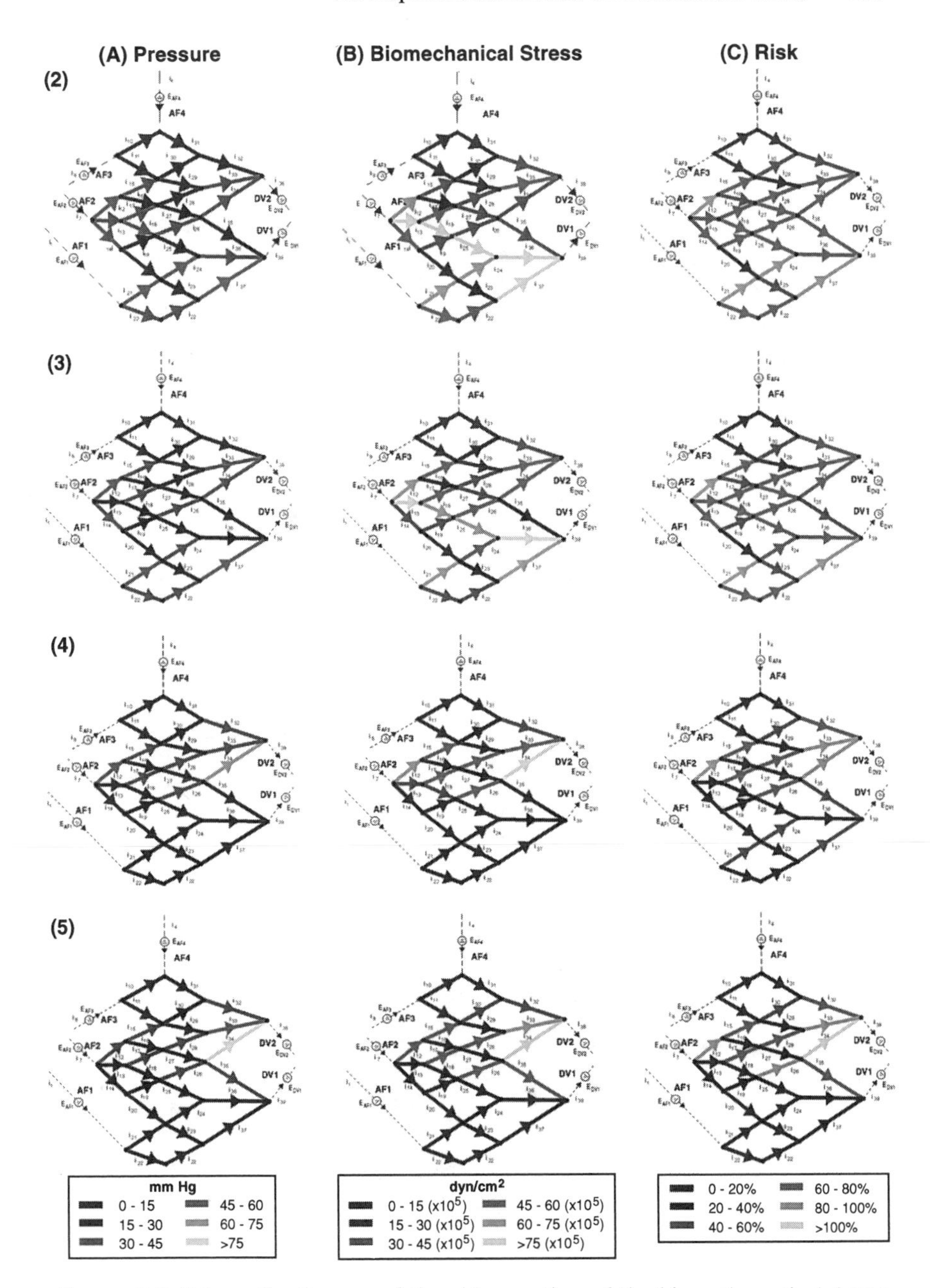

FIGURE 7.5. Schematic diagram of the nidus portion of the biomathematical AVM model (see also color insert that follows p. 170) depicting the intranidal values of (A) intravascular pressure gradient, (B) biomechanical stress, and (C) risk of rupture with draining vein (DV) 1 occluded 25%, 50%, 75%, and 100% and DV2 patent. The number along the left-hand column refers to the simulation number. (Reproduced, with permission, from *Stroke*, **27**, G.J. Hademenos and T.F. Massoud, Risk of intracranial arteriovenous malformation rupture due to venous drainage impairment: A theoretical analysis, pp. 1072–1083. © 1996 American Heart Association.)

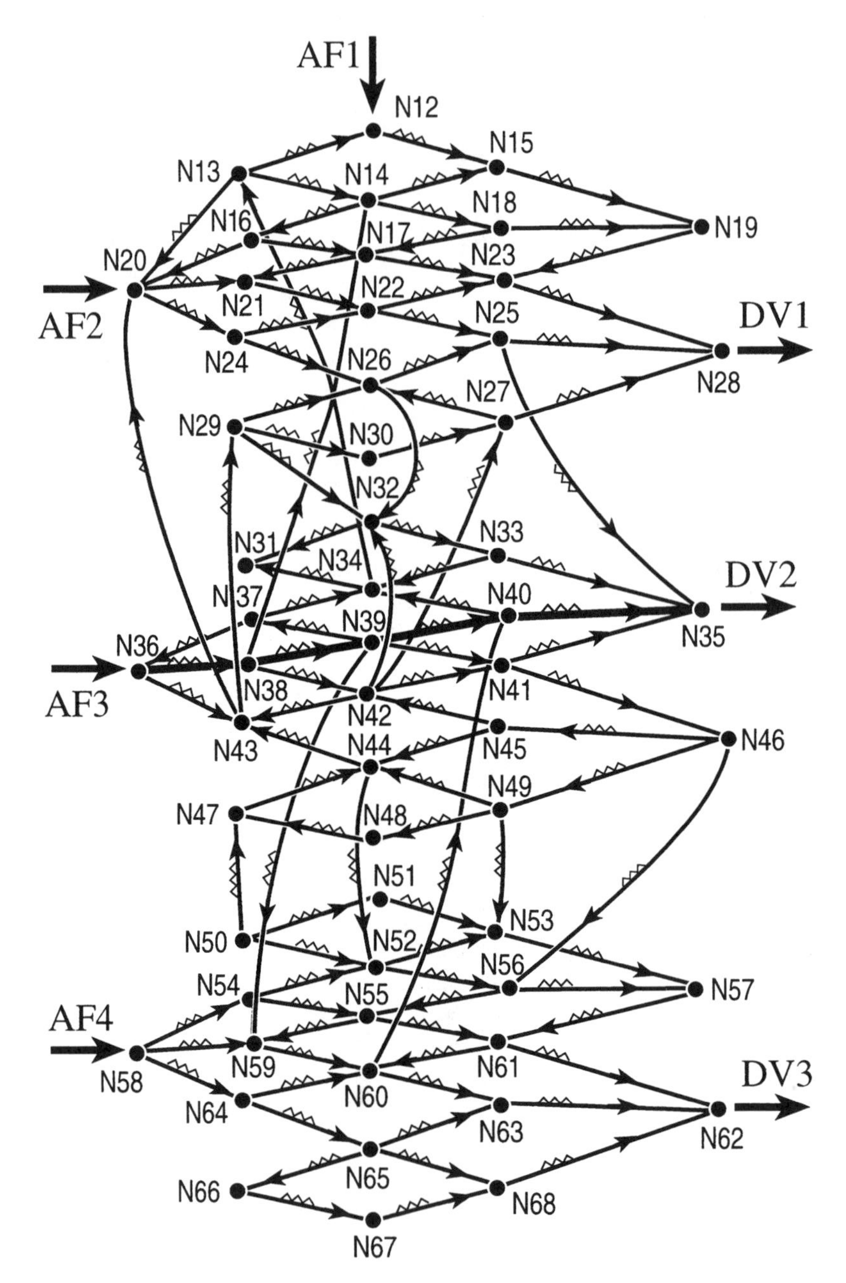

FIGURE 7.6. Schematic diagram of the electrical network describing the 3D biomathematical AVM model. AF, arterial feeder; DV, draining vein; N, node.

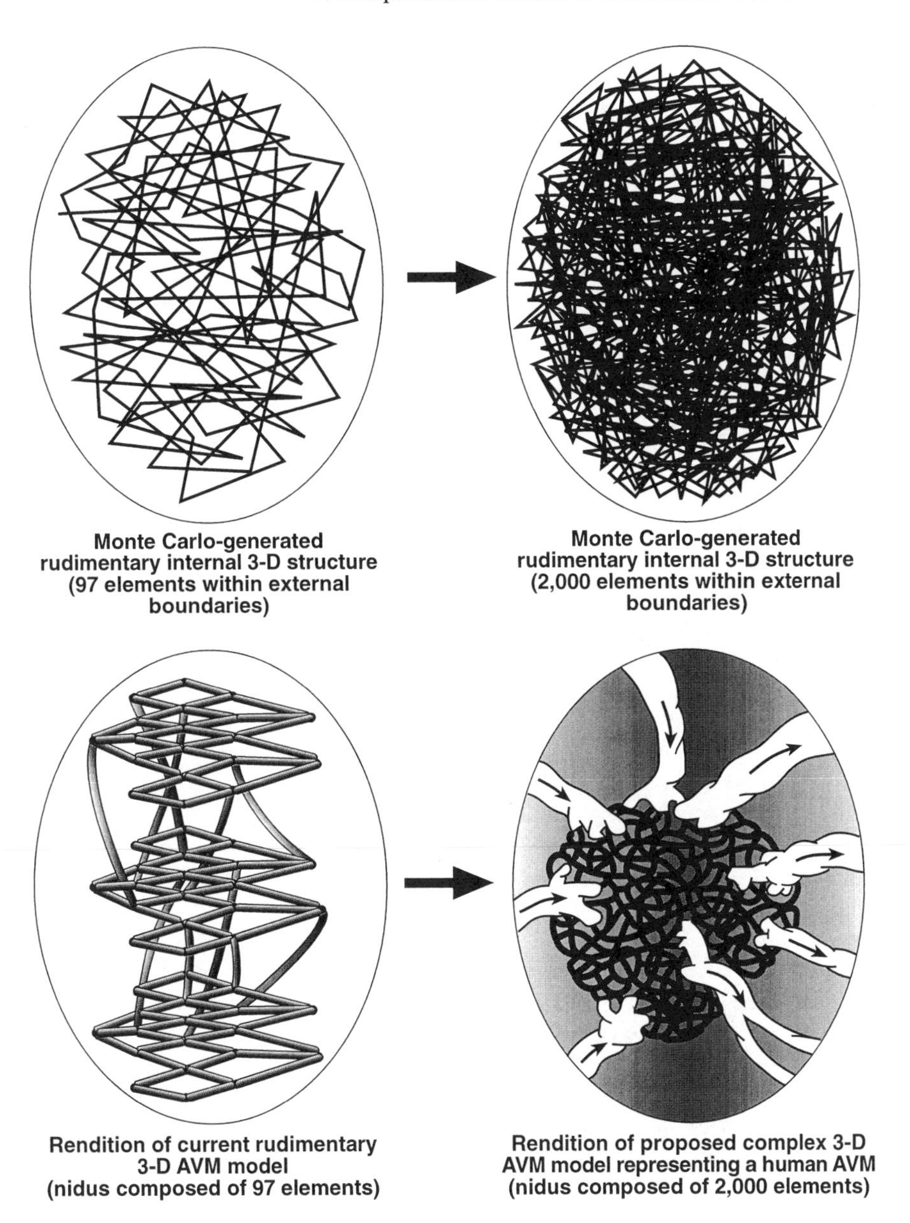

FIGURE 7.7. A schematic representation of Monte Carlo techniques for the development of a 3D electrical network intracranial AVM model.

plate according to the following parameters of the AVM nidus and value ranges: plexiform vessel radius 0.01–0.05 cm; plexiform vessel length 2–6 cm; fistulous vessel radius 0.1–0.2 cm; fistulous vessel length 3–5 cm; branching parameter of vessels: 0, terminal; 1, continuous; 2, bifurcation; 3, trifurcation; and vascular density or total number of nidus vessels.

3. The spatial coordinates and hemodynamic parameters of the AFs and DVs are assigned and implemented into the model. Hemodynamic simulations can now be performed by specifically designed programs to solve electrical networks. Quantitative information including angiographic, experimental, clinical, histological, and physiological can be used as input to guide the design of the nidus vessels and associated angioarchitecture, which is extremely difficult to elucidate using current imaging technology.

It is fully acknowledged that limitations are presented by the inability to obtain precise intranidal values of hemodynamic and biophysical parameters on a patient-by-patient basis. It is this limitation that prompts one to emphasize the potential role of the above proposed 3D (Biomathematical Model) AVM model in the management of patients with AVMs. The role of the biomathematical AVM model may serve as an additional objective measure upon which to base decisions regarding therapy, particularly in problematic cases where the AVM is either surgically inaccessible, large, or located in a deep or eloquent region of the brain. It would not be intended that the model supercede any and all factors employed currently in the decision process regarding therapy.

Example 4: Angiographic observations. Endovascular embolization is a technique that can be used to treat small AVMs completely or to reduce substantially the size of large AVMs through staged embolization prior to radiosurgery or neurosurgical resection. In either application, the AVM is assessed, both from a morphological and hemodynamic standpoint, with selective (SA) and superselective (SSA) angiography. SA involves injection of contrast medium in a major artery (usually the internal carotid or vertebral artery) proximal to the AVM and results in delineation of most or all of the nidus. In SSA, contrast medium injection is performed as close as possible to the AVM nidus through the AF, revealing anatomical, functional, and hemodynamic information regarding portions of the AVM and its surroundings, as shown in the angiograms of AVMs presented in Fig. 7.8. Knowledge of this infomation is crucial in determining the position, rate, and strategy of embolic agent injection, and the necessary polymerization time. The anatomical information revealed by SSA includes the distance of the microcatheter tip to the nidus, the presence of normal cortical side-branches or dysplastic aneurysms on the AF, intranidal angioarchitecture including presence of intranidal fistula(e) or aneurysms, and DV morphology. The dynamic information provided by SSA consists of a crude deter-

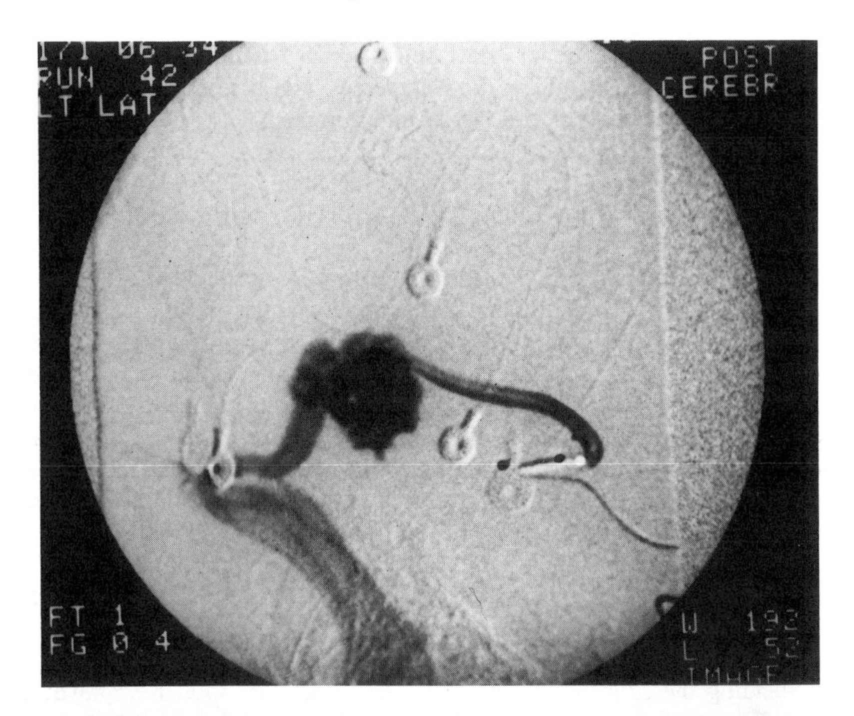

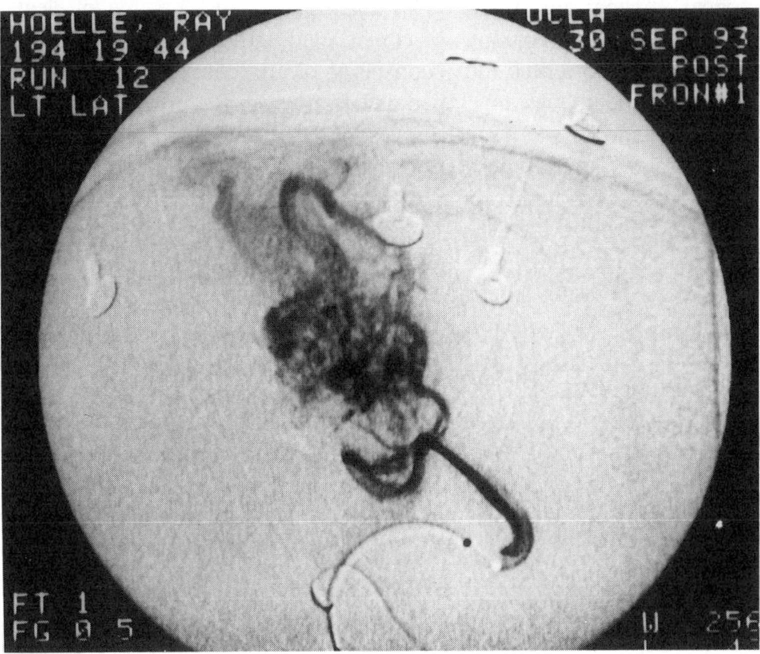

FIGURE 7.8. Angiograms of a (A) single feeder and (B) multiple feeder (superselective angiogram via one feeder) human arteriovenous malformation.

mination of the approximate arteriovenous transit time through the nidus, whereas the functional information gathered may arise consequent to the appearance of neurological deficits during or immediately after the injection of contrast medium or short-acting anesthetics such as Amytal. This may indicate the presence of angiographically occult branches to surrounding healthy brain and therefore may alert the operator to avoid injecting an embolic agent in that particular position of the AF.

Of additional significance is the further information provided by SSA that may be characterized as both anatomical and dynamic, that is, the spread of flow through and the extent of that portion of the nidus supplied by the particular AF through which the superselective angiogram is performed. The resultant delineation of the various intranidal compartments (vide infra) using SSA is a reflection on the morphological characteristics of the AF, nidus, and DV as outlined by SSA and on the hemodynamic balance present within the confines of the nidus. SA is a technique used primarily for the assessment of AVM presence, overall size, topography, and major anatomical landmarks, and the number and caliber of AFs and morphology of DVs, while SSA defines those angioarchitectural and dynamic features of nidus compartments that represent essential information for the performance and success of embolotherapy.

Extending the concept of the 2D electrical network model employed in the clinical applications described in Examples 1 and 2, a novel electrical network model of a cerebral AVM constructed with multiple AFs and DVs, and a 3D spatially oriented nidus consisting of interconnected plexiform and fistulous components was developed as described in the previous example.[70] The 3D AVM model was used to investigate intranidal hemodynamic compartmentalization as may be demonstrated by SSA and the effects of nidus angioarchitecture on the behavior of simulated contrast medium or embolic agent injected through the AFs.

Simulated SSA of the AVM nidus was performed by increasing the intravascular pressure (thus simulating a contrast medium injection pressure) within the major AFs proximal to the AVM. Superselective angiography was simulated through AF3 and AF4 by increasing the mean intravascular pressure within either AF by 10, 20, or 30 mm Hg while maintaining all the other AFs patent and at their normal pressure. The pressure changes within components of the nidus consequent to SSA were considered to represent the spread of contrast medium and hence the angiographic delineation of portions (compartments) of the nidus. The consequent intravascular pressure changes within each intranidal vessel downstream from the site of injection were determined using electrical network analysis. In reality, these calculated pressure alterations within nidus vessels are linearly related to the flow changes (in ml/min), and changes in either parameter could have been considered as representative of contrast filling of the nidus. These changes were reported as an average of all the percentage increases in intravascular pressure (relative to the normal baseline pressure) ($\Delta P\%$) for each individual

TABLE 7.2. Results of simulated superselective angiography through the major arterial feeders of the 3D biomathematical AVM model.

Inj. AF[a]	Injection pressure (mm Hg)	Extent (%)	ΔP^b (%)
AF3	10	87.6	14
AF3	20	88.7	20
AF3	30	89.7	57
AF4	10	25.8	11
AF4	20	27.8	19
AF4	30	34.0	30

[a] Inj. represents injection; AF, arterial feeder.
[b] ΔP is the average rise in intravascular pressure of the nidus vessels above baseline values.

nidus vessel, according to

$$(\%\ \text{Increase}\ \Delta P) = \frac{\displaystyle\sum_{nv=1}^{N} \frac{P_{\text{inj}} - P_{\text{bsln}}}{P_{\text{bsln}}}}{\sum \text{NV}_{\text{inj}}} \times 100\%,$$

where P_{inj} is the total intravascular pressure of the nidus vessel consequent to the injection in the AF, P_{bsln} is the baseline intravascular pressure prior to injection in the AF, NV_{inj} are the nidus vessels that experienced an increase in intravascular pressure, and N is an integer corresponding to the number of affected nidus vessels. Furthermore, the number of intranidal vessels affected by this increase in pressure consequent to the injection was reported as a percentage of the total number of nidus vessels.

Assessment of the effects of simulated SSA was evaluated by a quantitative tabulation of all intranidal vessels that experienced an increase in intravascular pressure and recorded as outlined above. These results are summarized in Table 7.2 and Figs. 7.9 and 7.10. SSA through the two major AFs resulted in the dissipation of IP (Injection Pressure) to different extents within the nidus, demonstrating, in effect, the presence of distinct intranidal hemodynamic compartments depending on which AF was injected. In SSA through AF3, which feeds into a trifurcation with one branch leading directly into the intranidal fistula, the intranidal dissipation of intravascular pressure occurred in 82 nidus vessels (87.6% of the nidus) at 10 mm Hg, and 86 nidus vessels (89.7% of the nidus) at 30 mm Hg above the baseline mean pressure of the AF. SSA through AF4 resulted in the dissipation of IP (Injection Pressure) in 25 nidus vessels (25.8% of the nidus) at 10 mm Hg and 34 nidus vessels (34.0% of the nidus) at 30 mm Hg above the baseline mean pressure. The average extent ($\Delta P\%$) to which these elevations in intravascular pressure occurred after SSA ranged from 14% at 10 mm Hg in-

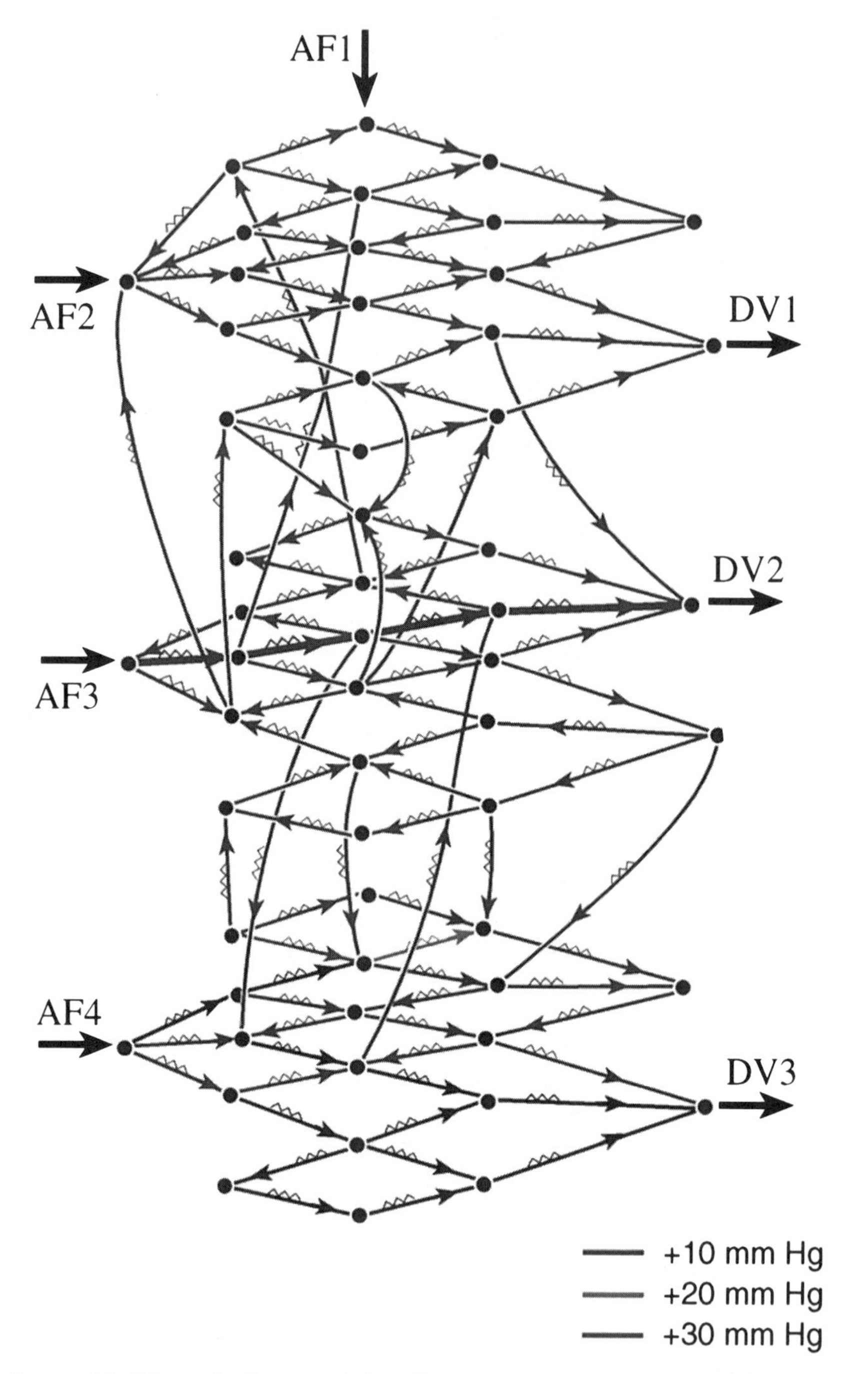

FIGURE 7.9. Schematic diagram of the nidus portion of the biomathematical AVM model (see also color insert that follows p. 170) simulating SSA through arterial feeder (AF) 3 at injection pressures of 10, 20, and 30 mm Hg represented by the color shaded regions.

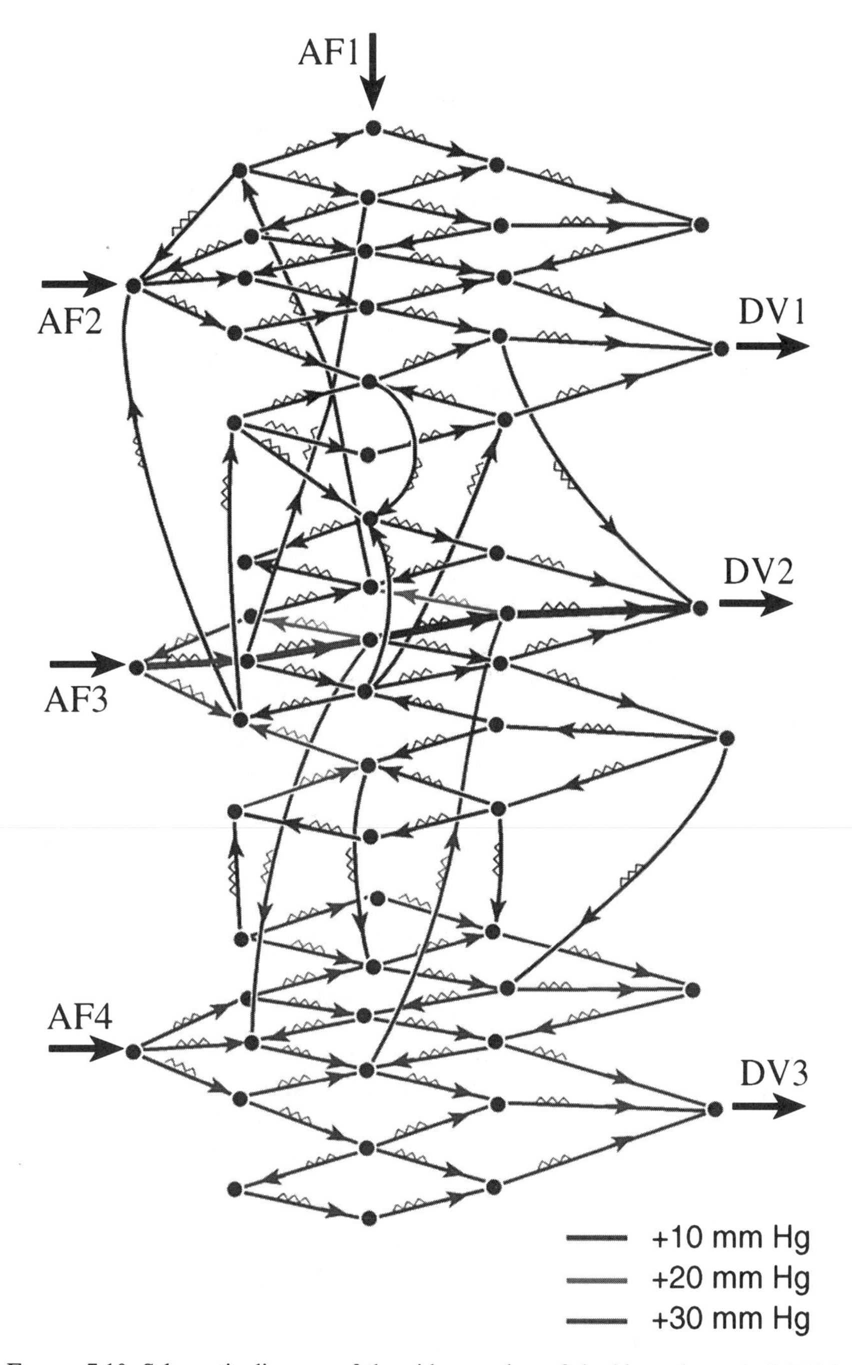

FIGURE 7.10. Schematic diagram of the nidus portion of the biomathematical AVM model (see also color insert that follows p. 170) simulating SSA through arterial feeder (AF) 4 at injection pressures of 10, 20, and 30 mm Hg represented by the color shaded regions.

jection pressure to 57% at 30 mm Hg injection pressure for injection through AF3 and from 11% at 10 mm Hg injection pressure to 30% at 30 mm Hg injection pressure for injection through AF4. Comparison of injections through AF3 and AF4 with a pressure of 10 mm Hg revealed a marked disparity in the influence of intranidal plexiform and fistulous vessels on the spread of simulated contrast medium—the fistula increased the dissemination of the injection pressure within the nidus to almost 100% of its volume. Comparison between the three simulations of SSA through AF3 shows minimal additional filling due to increase in injection pressure. Therefore, AVM angioarchitecture appears to be a more important factor than the injection in determining the spread through the nidus. Qualitative analysis of the overall size and extent of spread of intranidal hemodynamic compartments upon increasing injection pressures was possible from the schematic diagrams of the AVM nidus presented in Figs. 7.9 and 7.10.

Example 5: Assessment of therapeutic procedures and strategies. As stated earlier, AVMs are potentially fatal lesions that dictate an aggressive implementation of therapeutic intervention in order to completely remove or substantially reduce the risk of AVM nidus rupture. The primary objective in the treatment of AVMs is the complete obliteration of the AVM and a concurrent immediate and complete cessation of blood flow. Three methods currently employed for the treatment of AVMs include the following, alone or in combination: neurosurgical intervention, endovascular embolotherapy, and stereotactic radiosurgery. Of the three potential methods of therapy, the one that permits complete removal of the lesion and associated risks of rupture is neurosurgery. However, for reasons including inaccessibility, size, and patient safety, some AVMs, particularly large AVMs, cannot be removed surgically and must therefore be managed by alternative strategies. The commonest combination of therapy that has been shown to effectively treat AVMs is embolotherapy followed by surgery.[71–73]

Neurosurgical resection of the AVM remains the most effective method of treatment for the complete removal of the AVM nidus and the immediate elimination of the inherent risk of rupture. In surgery, the first step in the resection of the lesion is the identification of the major arterial feeders. Once the surgeon identifies the feeders, the surgeon carefully dissects around the volumetric boundary of the AVM, isolating the lesion from normal brain.[74] Occlusion of arterial feeders prior to draining veins is a conventional technique that is followed by most neurosurgeons during operative removal of intracranial AVMs. However, since draining veins are larger than the arterial feeders and readily identified from diagnostic images, the question arises as to the possibility or, more importantly, the safety of occluding, transecting, and mobilizing a draining vein (using it as a handle) as a first step toward dissection of the AVM core (Malis procedure[75]). It has been stated that this is permissible (safe) only in the presence of multiple veins draining an AVM, so as not to impair its total drainage with consequent nidus rupture. This was supported by the investigation of venous drainage impairment using the electrical network model (described in Example 2). Occlusion of the draining vein fed by the intranidal fistula induced AVM rupture while occlusion of the opposite vein, being fed by low-flow plexiform vessels, did not induce AVM rupture. Thus, should more than one draining vein be totally occluded before arterial feeders during surgery, then the risk of immediate rupture would depend on the ratio of number of draining veins to arterial feeders for that particular AVM. However, adopting the Malis procedure as originally conceived, i.e., occlusion of only one vein (the most hemodynamically appropriate) in the presence of multiple veins, would ensure as low a risk as possible of rupturing the AVM. Regardless of the surgical technique, neurosurgical resection is the only way to rapidly and completely excise the AVM.

The abrupt increase in cerebral perfusion pressure, particularly in adjacent regions of normal brain that has lost autoregulatory capacity, upon treatment (either embolization or surgery) may be involved in the pathogenesis of certain complications such as brain swelling or hemorrhage.[76–79] This is termed *normal perfusion pressure breakthrough*. In addition to the complications, disadvantages of neurosurgical intervention such as direct entrance into the cranial cavity, general anesthesia, the risk of post-operative infection, lengthy recovery time, and substantial cost directly foster and encourage trends toward alternative minimally invasive therapeutic approaches of AVMs. The electrical network model has been employed to investigate resultant hemodynamics and related mechanisms of nidus rupture presented by these minimally invasive therapies: endovascular embolotherapy and radiosurgery.

Endovascular Embolotherapy. The role of embolization in the treatment of AVMs is similar to that of aneurysms—reserved for problematic AVMs not readily accessible at surgery and pose a high risk to patient safety and subsequent outcome. Preoperative and intraoperative embolization can reduce the size and number of feeding pedicles, making subsequent surgical excision technically easier and safer.[80] In embolotherapy, a chemical or mechanical agent (embolic agent) is delivered to the AVM via the arterial feeders in an attempt to occlude the nidus and redirect blood flow to normal adjacent regions of the brain. The ideal embolic material for embolization of an AVM should (1) flow freely through the entire length of available delivery microcatheters; (2) lodge controllably and safely within the nidus, not passing through to the venous drainage or to the lungs; (3) cause complete and permanent occlusion of the nidus; (4) not induce a necrotizing vasculitis or vascular inflammatory response in the adjacent normal brain; and (5) ready availability.[66] Examples of embolic agents include short coils, glue, particles, and surgical silk suture.[81] The embolic agents are selectively injected via an arterial feeder and permeate a nidus volume dependent on the volume of agent, the injection pressure, and arterial flow.

Although the morbidity or mortality rates from embolotherapy continue to improve with the increasing experience of the neuroradiologist and advancements in technological instrumentation, complications do arise as a result of embolotherapy, possibly leading to AVM rupture. Seven possible mechanisms of AVM rupture during embolization include the following.[82]

1. High injection pressures required for the delivery into the nidus precipitating pressure rises in AFs. High surges in intranidal pressure as a result of the dissipation of elevated upstream arterial feeder injection pressures (during delivery of contrast medium and/or embolic agents) may result in AVM nidus rupture. This can be simulated in the AVM model by increasing incrementally the intravascular pressures of AF1 or AF2 to values of up to a clinially realistic maximum pressure, e.g., 50 mm Hg above baseline intravascular pressure for these feeders. The resulting AVM simulation, following each distinct increase in arterial feeder pressure, will provide hemodynamic values (blood flow, intravascular pressure, and risk of rupture) for all intranidal vessels situated downstream from the site of injection.
2. Possible uncontrollable deposition in the feeding artery or, if an intranidal fistula is present or fragmentation occurs, in the draining veins or lungs. The disastrous complication that occurs when embolic glue extends to and polymerizes within draining veins, resulting in immediate rupture of an AVM nidus, can be simulated by occluding DV1 totally in the presence of varying degrees of distal intranidal fistula occlusion. These schemes of vascular occlusion should be conceived so as to simulate the inadvertent extension of glue from the distal intranidal fistula to the main draining vein of the AVM during its embolization.
3. An induced vessel wall inflammatory response. Even though inflammatory response deals primarily with the biological reaction of the vessel wall, the resultant effect is the weakening of the vessel wall. The presence and degree of inflammation, in effect, lowers the elastic modulus of the affected vessels, making them much weaker and more prone to rupture.
4. Thrombus formation around the embolic agent, with subsequent natural thrombolysis and restoration of flow to a possibly weakened necrotic vessel.
5. Venous stasis and thrombosis with delayed AVM rupture. Flow reduction and delayed thrombosis of draining veins sufficient to induce venous outlet obstruction after partial AVM occlusion has been implicated as a further mechanism for AVM rupture complicating embolization. A number of patterns of vascular occlusion of the AVM model should be implemented that reflect varying extents of nidus (both plexiform and fistulous components) embolization and draining vein occlusion that could conceivably result in nidus rupture. In the conception of these embolization schemes, an attempt should be made to represent partially embolized AVMs by progressively increasing extents of nidus vessel occlusion. However, due to the presence of a fistula in this AVM, it can be reasoned that embolic glue would fill this path of least resistance preferentially, resulting in a nonuniform occlusion of the nidus. Therefore, simulations should be performed in

such a manner that simulated embolic glue would always occlude the distal aspect of the fistula to the same extent (percentage) as the more proximally situated plexiform vessels. It can also be reasoned that stasis and thrombosis of DV1 (that draining the fistula) would be much more significant than that of DV2 consequent to the occlusion of the distal portions of the intranidal fistula. Therefore, this simulated occlusion of the DVs should be weighted towards DV1, with thrombosis of DV2 only occurring once 50% of DV1 had thrombosed.

6. Obliteration of associated arteriovenous fistulae causing immediate redistribution into an AVM nidus. It has been suggested by Viñuela *et al.*[72] that abrupt embolic occlusion of an intranidal fistula may result in rerouting of blood flow through delicate plexiform vessels of a nidus, which may result in their immediate rupture. This speculative mechanism of intranidal redistribution of hemodynamic forces can be tested in the AVM model by occlusion of the four intranidal vessels comprising the fistula in a systematic fashion, individually and in all possible combinations that included adjoining fistulous vessels (while maintaining all plexiform vessels patent).

7. Another mechanism of AVM rupture during embolization is the rupture of intranidal aneurysms. The presence of these distinct lesions has a significant impact on strategies that are adopted for endovascular embolotherapy or radiosurgery. Usually, the primary goal is to either aggressively treat the aneurysm if located on an AF or embolize the AF directly connected to that part of the nidus containing the aneurysm first because the aneurysm is thin-walled and will lead to rupture if directly affected by changes in the intranidal hemodynamics consequent to the embolization procedure.[84,85] Theoretical implementation of this mechanism into the biomathematical model allows one to integrate information and knowledge from the biomathematical model of aneurysms discussed in Chap. 6.[86] Once the intravascular pressure has been solved for all nidus vessels throughout the electrical network, the pressure can be substituted into the aneurysm model as the intra-aneurysmal pressure. Using approximations for the other biophysical paramenters as was done previously, it becomes a simple task to determine the risk of rupture for an intranidal aneurysm.

These mechanisms of AVM rupture at embolotherapy are believed to be based, at least in part, to hemodynamics, the electrical network model serves as an important tool in the investigation of the role of hemodynamics in causing AVM rupture. For mechanism (1), high injection pressures can be implemented into the electrical network model by increasing the intravascular pressure of the particular arterial feeder through which the injection will occur to correspond to the injection pressure. Mechanisms (2) and (6) are related in that they involve occlusion of particular AVM nidus vessels, i.e., the fistula components and draining veins were explained in Example 2. Although the pathological processes responsible for rupture in mechanisms (3) and (4) are different, they conclude with the same result: a biomechanical weakening of the wall of the nidus vessel, making it more prone to rupture. Simulation of a weakened wall can be done with the electrical network model by reducing the elastic modulus and wall thickness of the nidus vessel in the risk of rupture calculations. Mechanism (5) first requires a simulated approximation of the dispersion of embolic agent upon injection through an arterial feeder. Obviously, it is known that injection through the feeder directly connected to the fistula will result in a larger permeation, but to what extent remains difficult to quantitate and thus speculative. In addition to the spread of embolic agent, one must adequately represent the systematic occlusion of the draining veins, which can be done according to the investigations presented previously. Mechanism (7) allows one to integrate information and knowledge from the biomathematical model of aneurysms discussed in Chapter 6.[86] Once the intravascular pressure has been solved for all nidus vessels throughout the electrical network, the pressure can be substituted into the aneurysm model as the intra-aneurysmal pressure. Using approximations for the other biophysical parameters as was done previously, it becomes a simple task to determine the risk of rupture for an intranidal aneurysm.

Throughout the course of this study, rupture was shown to occur in a selected number of simulations for each of the mechanisms of rupture. However, each simulation indicating rupture presented with two common, underlying characteristics: All involved the occlusion of the fistulous component and toward the venous end of the AVM nidus.

Radiosurgery. The term *radiosurgery* was proposed in 1951 by Leskell to describe a procedure that enables "brain fiber tracks to be sectioned and nuclei to be destroyed with high precision, without trephination, through the intact skull" using a high-dose, single fraction, stereotactically targeted radiation.[87] Steiner *et al.* proposed the radiosurgical treatment of intracranial AVMs, and in 1970, the first patient was selected.[88] Currently, three different types of penetrating radiation are in use: (a) protons or helium ions produced by a cyclotron or a synchrotron; (b) γ irradiation delivered by a 60 Co source (e.g., "gamma knife") and (c) x irradiation produced by a linear accelerator (LINAC). Regardless of the type of penetrating radiation, they all are ionizing and interact with matter (biological tissues) in the same manner. Each type of radiation induces an ionization or localized deposit of a large amount of energy into the AVM tissue, initiating a chain of events that ultimately leads to the biologic effect of vascular occlusion.[89] Since 1970, the overall role of stereotactic radiosurgery has been established in the management of carefully selected vascular malformations. By 1992, worldwide, more than 6000 patients had undergone stereotactic radiosurgery for AVMs.[90] At present, there are 150–200 facilities performing radiosurgery in North America, with brain AVMs being the commonest (32%) indication for radiosurgical treatment.[91]

Radiosurgery is a minimally invasive therapy of brain AVMs that represents one of the most useful adjuvants to conventional neurosurgery. Although radiosurgery continue to evolve with advancing technology, the risks of AVM rupture and ensuing neurological complications associated with these therapies are still present and remain a substantial concern. Optimal stereotactic radiosurgery for cerebral AVMs depends on accurate definition of the AVM nidus, precision in radiation delivery, a steep reduction in the radiation dose outside the nidus, and proper selection of the dose used.[92] Higher rates of complete AVM obliteration are seen in patients who (a) receive a higher radiation dose, (b) have smaller AVMs, (c) have the entire nidus treated, and (d) are younger.

In treating AVMs radiosurgically, the goal is to produce an inflammatory reaction in the vessel walls of the malformation by irradiating the constituent epithelial cells.[93] Radiation injury to the AVM vessels causes endothelial cell damage and proliferation, overproduction of elastic tissue, intima degeneration, media degeneration, and hyalin thickening, which leads to altered blood flow dynamics, hemostasis, and eventually thrombosis and obliteration of the AVM.[39] Complete AVM obliteration is observed when blood flow through the AVM has ceased and generally takes three years following radiosurgery to occur. Prior to complete obliteration, a latent period exists during which the irradiated nidus vessels begin to narrow with luminal obstruction resulting in potential hemodynamic disturbances predisposing to AVM nidus rupture. It is during this latent period, typically between six and nine months post radiosurgery, that the risk of AVM hemorrhage increases before falling exponentially to negligible levels. This is particularly the case for partially treated AVMs.[94] Complications from the radiosurgical treatement of AVMs arise from the radiation effects on the brain tissue, the degree of which is dependent on the radiation dosage and volume of tissue irradiation.

The electrical network AVM model was used to simulate the response of a theoretical intracranial AVM to radiosurgery with the application of two different hypothetical occlusive schemes to intranidal vessels.[95] The occlusion schemes (i.e., the schemes by which simulated vessels of an AVM nidus could undergo occlusion after irradiation) were based on three primary factors: mechanism of vessel occlusion, radiation dosage, and extent of irradiated AVM volume. Although the underlying mechanisms of vessel occlusion in response to radiation are speculative, two mechanisms have been proposed in the literature and are applied individually to the AVM model simulations described herein. These two mechanisms of vessel occlusion are (1) stepwise circumferential vessel narrowing and eventual occlusion, and (2) random immediate total vessel occlusion. In the first mechanism, the radius of each nidus vessel within the irradiated AVM volume was reduced abruptly by a uniform percentage of the initial vessel radius at discrete time intervals after simulated radiosurgery. The quantitative percentage values depended on the radiation dosage and the time lapsed post-irradiation and will be discussed below. The second mechanism of occlusion involves the total occlusion of nidus vessels randomly selected (using a random number generator) within the irradiated AVM volume according to the percentage of affected vessels dictated by the radiation dosage and time lapsed post-irradiation.

Both stepwise and random occlusion schemes were investigated in the electrical network AVM model simulations according to the two levels of radiation dosage D: (1) $D < 25$ gray (Gy) and (2) $D \geq 25$ Gy. The rate of occlusion is dependent strongly on the radiation dose delivered to the AVM volume as evidenced by the data presented by Yamamoto *et al.*[96] Using these data, the exact data points were recorded and fitted to polynomial functions through interpolation. The functions for each radiation dose are given below:

$$y = \begin{cases} \left(40 - \dfrac{14(-2+x)(-1+x)}{3}\right)x, & D < 25\ \text{Gy} \\ \left[88 + \left(-38 + 32\,\dfrac{-2+x}{3}\right)(-1+x)\right]x, & D \geq 25\ \text{Gy} \end{cases}$$

where x is the time post-radiosurgery and y is the percent occlusion.

Investigations of the effects of radiosurgery on irradiated AVM volume were performed through simulations of the occlusion schemes on the total nidus (complete treatment), the upper and lower halves (UH, LH) of the nidus, and four quarters (Q1–Q4) of the nidus (partial treatment), as shown in Fig. 7.11.

The results from the application of the electrical network model to radiosurgery are summarized in Table 7.3. Four (14.3%) out of a total 28 sets of AVM radiosurgery simulations revealed theoretical nidus rupture ($R_{\text{rupt}} \geq 100\%$). Three of these were associated with partial nidus coverage, and one with complete treatment. All ruptured AVMs had received low-dose radiosurgery. Intranidal hemodynamic perturbations were observed in all cases of AVM rupture; the occlusion of a fistulous component resulted in intranidal re-routing of flow and escalation of the intravascular pressure in adjacent plexiform components leading to their rupture.

The theoretical rates of AVM hemorrhage after radiosurgery are low, particularly when radiation-induced fibrosis of nidus vessels is considered. However, intranidal hemodynamic perturbations may result from partial or complete radiosurgery, contributing to their rupture during the latency period. This study confirms the danger of subtotal and low-dose AVM radiosurgery.

It was concluded that intranidal hemodynamic perturbations may result theoretically from partial and complete radiosurgery of AVMs, contributing to the rupture during the latency period. The higher incidence of rupture after partial irradiation confirms the danger of subtotal AVM treatment. The radiosurgical occlusion of intranidal fistulae or larger-caliber plexiform

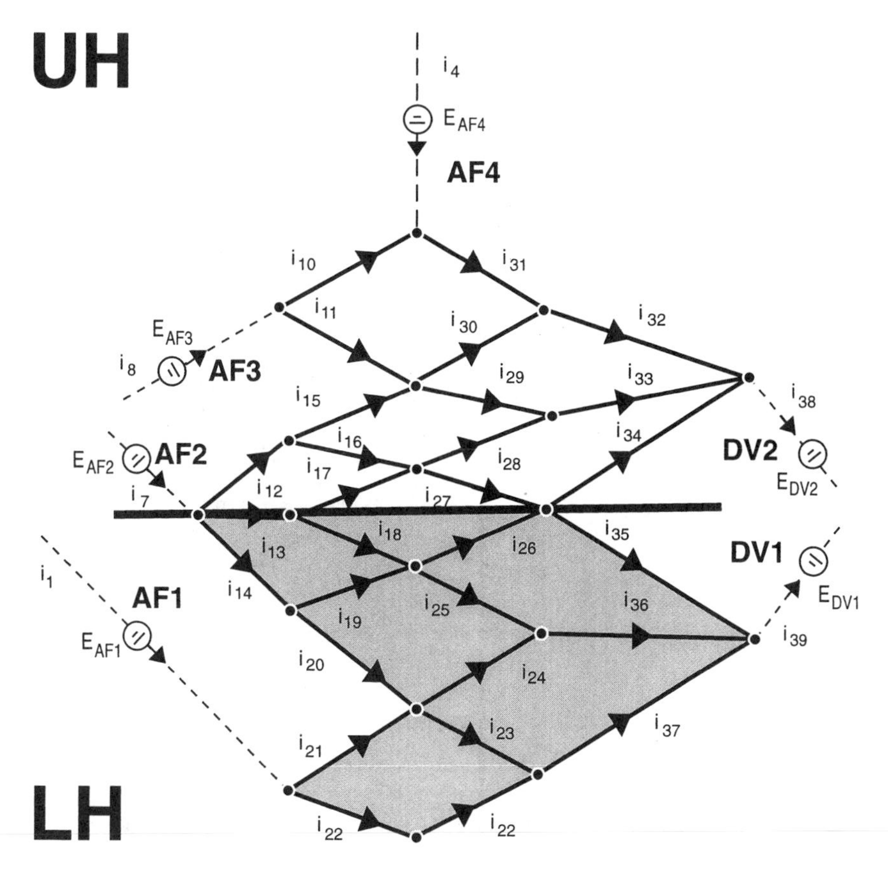

FIGURE 7.11. Schematic diagram of the nidus portion of the electrical network AVM model corresponding to the extent of nidus subjected to radiosurgery.

vessels appears to be the main culprit in the generation of critical intranidal hemodynamic surges that result in nidus rupture.

This section presented many illustrative examples and clinical applications of a biomathematical model to scientific and clinical investigations of intracranial AVMs. In fact, of all of the available computational and laboratory resources, biomathematical models exhibit a great potential in advancing current knowledge of AVMs limited only by creativity, imagination, and ingenuity.

7.5 Management of Intracranial AVMs

Upon diagnosis, the attending physician must assimilate a host of mitigating hemodynamic and biophysical factors upon which to assess the stability of the AVM and ultimately decide on the optimal course of treatment. The

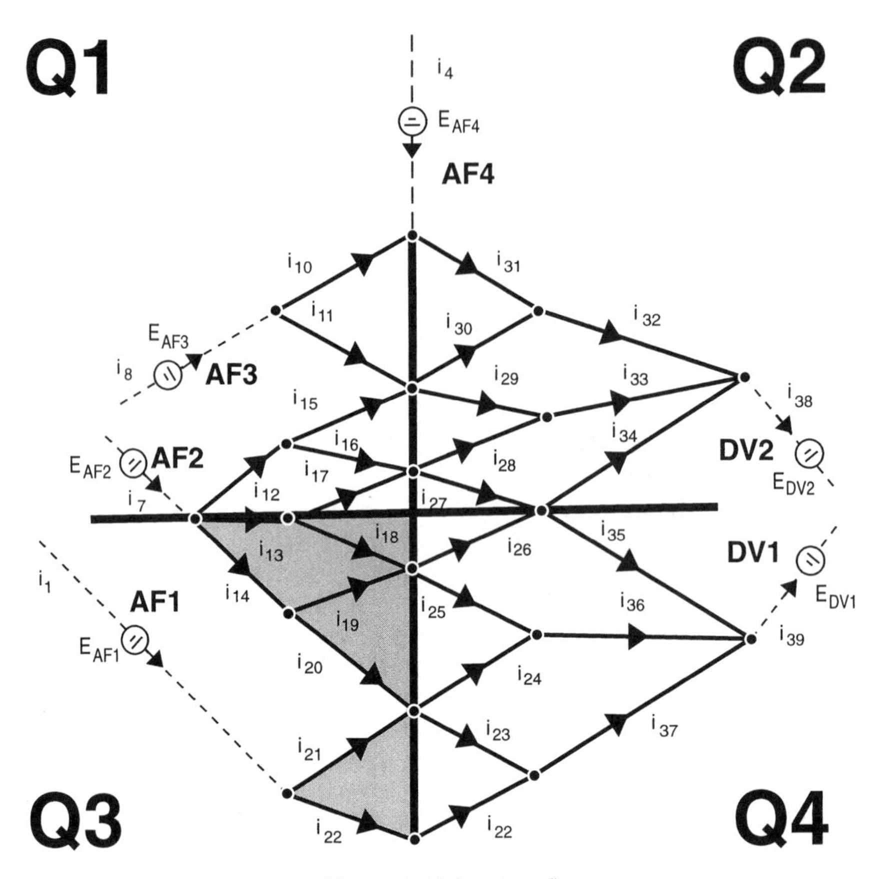

FIGURE 7.11 (*continued*)

primary objective in the management of intracranial AVMs is the prevention of hemorrhage and consequent complications. Although statistical studies have been performed identifying angioarchitectural or structural features of an AVM that are highly corrrelated with rupture,[97–99] each patient presents a unique case, making it extremely difficult if not impossible to accurately quantify the risk of a particular AVM to rupture for a given patient. To illustrate this uniqueness, Kader *et al.*[97] investigated specifically the venous drainage of AVM patients and concluded that a single draining vein, severely impaired venous drainage, and deep venous drainage were associated with hemorrhage. Turjman *et al.*[98] found that AVM factors associated with hemorrhage were deep venous drainage, feeding by perforators, intranidal aneurysms, multiple aneurysms feeding by the vertebrobasilar system, and location in the basal ganglia. Pollock *et al.*[99] observed that the factors associated with hemorrhage included history of a prior bleed, a single draining vein, and diffuse AVM morphology. Given this degree of variability, the general attitude in the management of patients afflicted with

TABLE 7.3. Summary of results from radiosurgical simulations of the theoretical AVM model for cases of nidus rupture (i.e., risk ⩾100%).

	Occlusion scheme		Dose			Time, vessel, and location of nidus rupture		
Case	R[a]	SW[b]	<25 Gy	⩾25 Gy	Extent of nidus irradiation[c]	Time[d]	Vessel[e]	Location
1	+		+		T	1 yr, 3 mo	21	A
2	+		+		LH	9 mo	14	A
3	+		+		Q3	9 mo	12	A
4	+		+		Q4	6 mo	37	V

[a] R represents random vascular occlusion scheme.
[b] SW represents step wise vascular occlusion scheme.
[c] T is total nidus; UH, upper half of the nidus; LH, lower half of the nidus; Q1,upper left quadrant of the nidus; Q2, upper right quadrant of the nidus; Q3, lower left quadrant of the nidus; Q4, lower right quadrant of the nidus.
[d] yr represents year; mo represents months.
[e] Specific nidus vessel in AVM model.
[f] Location, nidus region: A, nidus region near the arterial feeders, and V, nidus region near the draining veins. Baseline (pretreatment) risk of rupture values for vessels 12, 14, 21, and 37 are 86.2%, 74.3%, 89.65, and 91.1%, respectively.

AVMs is toward an aggressive therapeutic approach, since these lesions are regarded as inherently dangerous, occurring in a young and productive age group in which hemorrhage can be severely incapacitating or fatal.[2]

In addition to the patient's medical history and results from laboratory investigations, factors specific to the AVM that guide decisions of management and therapy include the following:

1. *AVM size*. The size of an AVM is an important factor in assessing the propensity of an AVM to rupture. Small AVMs (≤3 cm in diameter) have been shown to rupture more frequently than larger AVMs.

2. *Location of AVM*. The location of an AVM has less to due with its likelihood to rupture and more to do in guiding therapeutic options. The possible locations of an AVM are demarcated as superficial (toward the surface of the brain) or deep (toward the center of the brain). Superficial AVMs can be reached easily through surgical intervention. Deep AVMs require a substantial amount of consideration with regard to treatment and may be referred for embolization or radiosurgery (discussed below). In addition, several regions of the brain, known as eloquent areas, are responsible for extremely important and sometimes life-sustaining function. Therapy for an AVM, particularly invasive procedures such as neurosurgical resection, would place the patient at high risk for permanent neurological deficit and a drastic reduction in the quality of life. At this stage of patient management, other adjuvant therapies are considered such as radiosurgery and embolotherapy (discussed below).

3. *Number and distribution of feeding arteries.* The role of feeding arteries on AVM rupture arise in assessing the supply of blood to a nidus and subsequent approaches to therapeutic obliteration. If an AVM consists of one or two feeders, they can be identified angiographically and permanently occluded at surgery, making removal of the lesion a simpler task. An increase in the number of feeders increases the difficulty of surgery and the probability that, should a residual portion of the nidus be overlooked at surgery, hemodynamic forces would still be exerted on a retained nidus, which still could rupture.

4. *Status and patterns of venous drainage.* Venous drainage impairment has been shown theoretically to induce rupture toward the venous side of the AVM and is dependent on the nidus angioarchitecture and hemodynamics, particularly if the draining vein is fed by an intranidal fistula.[14] Occlusion of such a draining vein induces a rapid redistribution of blood into the weak plexiform vessels of the opposing region of the nidus causing a hemodynamic overload and an increased risk of rupture. There are, in essence, two patterns of venous drainage, deep and superficial.

5. *Number and distribution of arterial feeders.* With regard to distribution, arterial feeders could be attached to the nidus either directly or indirectly through much smaller arterial shunts. A direct feeder provides direct access to the nidus and complete stoppage of flow upon occlusion. The small size of the arterial shunts makes it likely that several feeder vessels, still supplying blood to the AVM, could be overlooked during therapy.

Given the complexity of an AVM presented with each case, theoretical approaches for the management of unruptured AVMs and assessment of intranidal stability have been proposed to determine and approximately quantitate the simulated risk of rupture based on previously existing data. In one method, management of unruptured AVMs is simulated theoretically using statistical or stochastic methods for a decision-tree analysis.[100,101] Regardless of the number or type of factors implemented in decision analysis, the conclusions tend to always indicate support for surgical intervention as the optimal choice of therapy. Another method is a mathematical derivation proposed by Kondziolka, McLaughlin, and Kesle[102] using the multiplicative law of probability:

$$\begin{aligned}&(\text{Risk of hemorrhage})\\&\quad= 1 - (\text{Risk of no hemorrhage})^{(\text{expected years of remaining life})}\end{aligned}$$

which requires only knowledge of patient age and annual hemorrhage risk. The above equation is based on life expectancy tables or tabular summaries of life expectancy of AVM patient populations compiled according to ranges of age. In another method of risk assessment of AVM rupture, Hademenos and Massoud derived a theoretical relation in terms of systemic and AVM pressures based on intranidal hemodynamics,[14] as expressed previously in Eq. (7.16). Methods designed to assess risk of AVM hemorrhage are not uniformly accepted as an ideal technique applicable to all patients with physicians opting instead, generally, to rely on past experiences to guide decisions regarding therapy.

7.6 Summary

Arteriovenous malformations comprise a large number of cases responsible for hemorrhagic stroke in the younger population, putting them at extreme risk for neurological complications and permanent deficits. AVMs are believed to be congenital in nature and represent, in essence, an abnormal capillary bed, providing a direct shunt for blood from the arterial circulation to the venous circulation. Knowledge of the biophysical and hemodynamic interactions and their role in the development and rupture of intracranial arteriovenous malformations has significantly advanced current understanding in the management of AVMs and serves as the basis for improved techniques in the diagnosis and therapy of arteriovenous malformations. The primary strategy in AVM treatment is to divert blood flow from the AVM to the surrounding normal cerebral circulation. Several options exist for treating AVMs including neurosurgical resection, embolotherapy, and radiosurgery used alone or in combination.These three techniques, particularly embolotherapy[103,104] and radiosurgery,[105,106] have advanced significantly due to the enormous strides in the knowledge of the biophysics and hemodynamics of AVMs. With the development and application of more complex biomathematical models and in vitro hydraulic models[107] of AVMs, one possesses the ability to simulate intranidal hemodynamics and accurately assess the propensity of an AVM to rupture. In addition, advancing technology and improved techniques for the treatment of AVMs are reducing the morbidity and mortality rates and improving the patient's outcome and overall quality of life.

7.7 References

1. R.H. Wilkins, "Natural history of intracranial vascular malformations: A review," Neurosurgery **16**, 421–430 (1985).
2. V.B. Graves and T.A. Duff "Intracranial arteriovenous malformations: Current imaging and treatment," Invest. Radiol. **25**, 952–960 (1990).
3. B.M. Stein, "General techniques for the surgical removal of arteriovenous malformations, in *Intracranial Arteriovenous Malformations*, edited by C.B. Wilson and B.M. Stein (Williams & Wilkins, Baltimore, 1992), pp. 143–155.
4. F. Turjman, T.F. Massoud, J.W. Sayre, F. Viñuela, G. Guglielmi, and G. Duckwiler, "Epilepsy associated with cerebral arteriovenous malformations: A multivariate analysis of angioarchitectural characteristics," Amer. J. Neuroradiol. **16**, 345–350 (1995).

5. B.M. Stein, S.M. Wolpert, "Arteriovenous malformations of the brain. II: Current concepts and treatment," Arch. Neurol. **37**, 69–75 (1980).
6. H.H. Branham, "Aneurysmal varix of the femoral artery and vein following a gunshot wound," Int J. Surg. **3**, 250 (1890).
7. E. Holman, *Abnormal Arteriovenous Communications* (Charles C. Thomas, Springfield, Ill, 1968), p. 14.
8. D.E. Strandness, Jr., *Peripheral Arterial Disease: A Physiologic Approach* (Little, Brown, Boston, 1969), Chap. 13, pp. 235–252.
9. D.E. Strandness, Jr., and D.S. Sumner, "Arteriovenous fistulas," in *Hemodynamics for Surgeons* (Grune & Stratton, Orlando, 1975).
10. K. Binak, *et al.*, "Arteriovenous fistula: Hemodynamic effects of occlusion and exercise," Am. Heart J. **60**, 495 (1960).
11. C.W. Frank, *et al.*, "An experimental study of the immediate hemodynamic adjustments to acute arteriovenous fistulae of various sizes," J. Clin. Invest. **34**, 772 (1955).
12. W.B. Hamby, "The pathology of supratentorial angiomas," J. Neurosurg. **22**, 65–75 (1957).
13. G, Duckwiler, J. Dion, F. Viñuela, B. Jabour, N. Martin, and J. Bentson, "Intravascular microcatheter pressure monitoring: Experimental results and early clinical evaluation," Amer. J. Neuroradiol. **11**, 169–175 (1990).
14. G.J. Hademenos and T.F. Massoud, "Risk of intracranial arteriovenous malformation rupture due to venous drainage impairment: A theoretical analysis," Stroke **27**, 1072–1083 (1996).
15. R.F. Spetzler and J.M. Zabramski, "Grading and staged resection of cerebral arteriovenous malformations," Clin. Neurosurg. **36**, 318–337 (1988).
16. A. Pasqualin, G. Barone, F. Cioffi, L. Rosta, R. Scienza, and R. Da Pian, "The relevance of anatomic and hemodynamic factors to a classification of cerebral arteriovenous malformations," Neurosurgery **28**, 370–379 (1991).
17. B. Pertuiset, D. Ancri, and F. Clergue, "Preoperative evaluation of hemodynamic factors in cerebral arteriovenous malformations for selection of a radical surgery tactic with special reference to vascular autoregulation disorders," Neurol. Res. **4**, 209–233 (1982).
18. S. Yamada, E.S. Brauer, and D.S. Knierim, "Direct approach to arteriovenous malformations in functional areas of the cerebral hemisphere," J. Neurosurg. **72**, 418–425 (1990).
19. M.G. Yasargil, "Surgical concerns," in *Microneurosurgery*, edited by M.G. Yasargil (Georg Thieme, New York, 1988), Vol. III B(IV), pp. 25–53.
20. W. Hassler and H. Steinmetz, "Cerebral hemodynamics in angioma patients: An intraoperative study," J. Neurosurg. **67**, 822–831 (1987).
21. W. Hassler, "Hemodynamic aspects of cerebral angiograms," Acta Neurochir. Suppl. **37**, 1–136 (1986).
22. H. Nornes and A. Grip, "Hemodynamic aspects of cerebral arteriovenous malformations," J. Neurosurg. **53**, 456–464 (1980).
23. H. Nornes, A. Grip, and P. Wikeby, "Intraoperative evaluation of cerebral hemodynamics using directional Doppler technique. Part 1: Arteriovenous malformations," J. Neurosurg. **50**, 145–151 (1979).
24. R. Leblanc and J.R. Little, "Hemodynamics of arteriovenous malformations," Clin. Neurosurg. **36**, 299–317 (1988).
25. A. Kader, W.L. Young, J. Pile-Spellman, H. Mast, R.R. Sciacca, J.P. Mohr,

B.M. Stein, The Columbia University AVM Study Project, "The influence of hemodynamic and anatomic factors on hemorrhage from cerebral arteriovenous malformations," Neurosurgery **34**, 801–808 (1994).

26. S. Yamada, S. Thio, R.P. Iacono, B.S. Yamada, F.S. Brauer, W. Hayward, V.J. Morgese, and M. Moghtader, "Total blood flow to arteriovenous malformations," Neurol. Res. **15**, 379–383 (1993).
27. I.F. Manchola, A.A.F. De Salles, T.K. Foo, R.H. Ackerman, G.T. Candia, and R.N. Kjellberg, "Arteriovenous malformation hemodynamics: A transcranial Doppler study," Neurosurgery **33**, 556–562 (1993).
28. R.R. Diehl, H. Henkes, H-C. Nasher, D. Kuhne, and P. Berlit, "Blood flow velocity and vasomotor reactivity in patients with arteriovenous malformations: A transcranial Doppler study," Stroke **25**, 1574–1580 (1994).
29. B.R. Rosenblum, R.F. Bonner, and E.H. Oldfield, "Intraoperative measurement of cortical blood flow adjacent to cerebral AVM using laser Doppler velocimetry," J. Neurosurg. **66**, 396–399 (1987).
30. T. Okabe, J.S. Meyer, H. Okayasu, R. Harper, J. Rose, R.G. Grossmann, R. Centeno, H. Tachibana, and Y.Y. Lee, "Xenon-enhanced CT CBF measurements in cerebral AVMs before and after excision: Contributions to pathogenesis and treatment," J. Neurosurg. **59**, 21–37 (1983).
31. R.W. Homan, M.D. Devous, E.M. Stokely, and F.J. Bonte, "Quantification of intracerebral steal in patients with arteriovenous malformation," Arch. Neurol. **43**, 779–785 (1986).
32. H. Mast, J.P. Mohr, A. Osipov, J. Pile-Spellman, R.S. Marshall, R.M. Lazar, B.M. Stein, W.L. Young, " 'Steal' is an unestablished mechanism for the clinical presentation of cerebral arteriovenous malformations," Stroke **26**, 1215–1220 (1995).
33. E.H. Lo, "A hemodynamic analysis of intracranial arteriovenous malformations," Neurol. Res. **15**, 51–55 (1993).
34. W.L. Young, J. Pile-Spellman, I. Prohovnik, A. Kader, B.M. Stein, and the Columbia University AVM Study Project, "Evidence for adaptive autoregulatory displacement in hypotensive cortical territories adjacent to arteriovenous malformations," Neurosurgery **34**, 601–611 (1994).
35. L. Hacien-Bey, R. Nour, J. Pile-Spellman, R. Van Heertum, P.D. Esser, and W.L. Young, "Adaptive changes of autoregulation in chronic cerebral hypotension with arteriovenous malformations: An acetazolamide-enhanced single-photon emission CT study," Amer. J. Neuroradiol. **16**, 1865–1874 (1995).
36. E. Ornstein, W.B. Blesser, W.L. Young, and J. Pile-Spellman, "A computer simulation of the haemodynamic effects of intracranial arteriovenous malformation occlusion," Neurol. Res. **16**, 345–352 (1994).
37. R.J. White, D.G. Fitzjerrell, and R.C. Croston, "Fundamentals of lumped compartmental modelling of the cardiovascular system," Adv. Cardiovasc. Phys. **5** (Part I), 162–184 (1983).
38. E.H. Lo, "A theoretical analysis of hemodynamics and biomechanical alterations in intracranial AVMs after radiosurgery," Int. J. Radiat. Oncol. Biol. Phys. **27**, 353–361 (1993).
39. E.H. Lo, J.I. Fabrikant, R.P. Levy, M.H. Phillips, K.A. Frankel, and E.L. Alpen, "An experimental compartmental flow model for assessing the hemodynamic response of intracranial arteriovenous malformations to stereotactic radiosurgery," Neurosurgery **28**, 251–259 (1991).

40. S.T. Hecht, J.A. Horton, and C.W. Kerber, "Hemodynamics of the central nervous system arteriovenous malformation nidus during particulate embolization: A computer model," Neuroradiology **33**, 62–64 (1991).
41. G.J. Hademenos, T.F. Massoud, and F. Viñuela, "A biomathematical model of intracranial arteriovenous malformations based on network analysis: Theory and hemodynamics," Neurosurgery **38**, 1005–1015 (1996).
42. F. Viñuela, "Endovascular therapy of brain arteriovenous malformations," Semin. Interventional Radiol. **5**, 269–280 (1987).
43. J-S. Lee, and T.C. Skalak, editors, *Microvascular Mechanics: Hemodynamics of Systemic and Pulmonary Microcirculation* (Springer, New York, 1989).
44. A.S. Popel, and P.C. Johnson, editors, *Microvascular Networks: Experimental and Theoretical Studies.* (Karger, New York, 1986).
45. J.E. Fletcher, "Mathematical modeling of the microcirculation," Math. Biosci. **38**, 159–202 (1978).
46. J.F. Gross, "The significance of pulsatile microhemodynamics," in *Microcirculation*, edited by G. Kaley and B.M. Altura (University Park Press, Baltimore, 1977), Vol. 1, Chap. 17, pp. 365–390.
47. J.F. Gross, M. Intaglietta, and B.W. Zweifach, "Network model of pulsatile hemodynamics in the microcirculation of the rabbit omentum," Am. J. Physiol. **226**, 1117–1123 (1974).
48. J.F. Gross, and J. Aroesty, "Mathematical models of capillary flow: A critical review," Biorheology **9**, 225–264 (1972).
49. D. Halliday, and R. Resnick, *Fundamentals of Physics*, 2nd ed. (Wiley, New York, 1981), Chap. 29.
50. M.D. Szabo, G. Crosby, P. Sundaram, B.A. Dodson, R.N. Kjellberg, "Hypertension does not cause spontaneous hemorrhage of intracranial arteriovenous malformations," Anesthesiology **70**, 761–763 (1989).
51. W.L. Young, A. Kader, J. Pile-Spellman, E. Ornstein, B.M. Stein, and the Columbia University AVM Study Project, "Arteriovenous malformation draining vein physiology and determinants of transnidal pressure gradients," Neurosurgery **35**, 389–396 (1994).
52. G.J. Hademenos, and T.F. Massoud, "An electrical network model of intracranial arteriovenous malformations: Analysis of variations in hemodynamic and biophysical parameters," Neurol. Res. **18**, 575–589 (1996).
53. P. Albert, H. Salgado, M. Polaina, F. Trujillo, A. Ponce de León, and F. Durand, "A study on the venous drainage of 150 cerebral arteriovenous malformations as related to hemorrhagic risks and size of the lesion," Acta Neurochir. (Wein) **103**, 30–34 (1990).
54. H-G. Höllerhage, "Venous drainage system and risk of hemorrhage from AVMs" (Letter), J. Neurosurg **77**, 652–653 (1992).
55. Y. Miyasaka, K. Yada, T. Ohwada, T. Kitahara, A. Kurata, and K. Irikura, "An analysis of the venous drainage system as a factor in hemorrhage from arteriovenous malformations," J. Neurosurg. **76**, 239–242 (1992).
56. Y. Miyasaka, A. Kurata, K. Tokiwa, R. Tanaka, K. Yada, and T. Ohwada, "Draining vein pressure increases and hemorrhage in patients with arteriovenous malformations," Stroke **25**, 504–507 (1994).
57. C.B. Wilson, and G. Hieshima, "Occlusive hyperemia: A new way to think about an old problem," J. Neurosurg. **78**, 165–166 (1993).
58. N.R.F. Al-Rodhan, T.M. Sundt, D.G. Piepgras, D.A. Nichols, D. Rüfenacht, and L.N. Stevens, "Occlusive hyperemia: A theory for the hemodynamic com-

plications following resection of intracerebral arteriovenous malformations," J. Neurosurg. **78**, 167–175 (1993).
59. M.K. Morgan, R.E. Anderson, and T.M. Sundt, "A model of the pathophysiology of cerebral arteriovenous malformations by a carotid-jugular fistula in the rat," Brain Res. **496**, 241–250 (1989).
60. J.M. Herman, R.F. Spetzler, J.B. Bederson, J.M. Kurbat, and J.M. Zabramski, "Genesis of a dural arteriovenous malformation in a rat model," J. Neurosurg. **83**, 539–545 (1995).
61. R.F. Spetzler *et al.*, "Normal perfusion pressure breakthrough theory," Clin. Neurosurg. **25**, 651–672 (1978).
62. T. Sakaki *et al.*, "Perfusion pressure breakthrough threshold of cerebral autoregulation in the chronically ischemic brain: An experimental study in cats," J. Neurosurg. **76**, 478–485 (1992).
63. R. Spiegelmann, W.A. Friedman, F.J. Bova, D.P. Theele, and J.P. Mickle, "LINAC radiosurgery: An animal model," J. Neurosurg. **78**, 638–644 (1993).
64. T.F. Massoud, C. Ji, F. Viñuela, G. Guglielmi, J. Robert, G.R. Duckwiler, and Y.P. Gobin, "An experimental arteriovenous malformation model in swine: Anatomic basis and construction technique," Amer. J. Neuroradiol. **15**, 1537–1545 (1994).
65. T.F. Massoud, C. Ji, F. Viñuela, F. Turjman, G. Guglielmi, G.R. Duckwiler, and Y.P. Gobin, "Laboratory simulations and training in endovascular embolotherapy with a swine arteriovenous malformation model," Amer. J. Neuroradiol. **17**, 271–279 (1996).
66. T.F. Massoud, C. Ji, G. Guglielmi, and F. Viñuela, "Endovascular treatment of arteriovenous malformations by selective intranidal occlusion with detachable platinum electrodes: Technical feasibility in animal models," Amer. J. Neuroradiol. **17**, 1459–1466 (1996).
67. P. Lylyk *et al.*, "Use of a new mixture for embolization of intracranial vascular malformations: Preliminary experimental experience," Neuroradiology **32**, 304–310 (1990).
68. J.C. Chaloupka, F. Viñuela, J. Robert, and G.R. Duckwiler, "An in vivo arteriovenous malformation model in swine: Preliminary feasibility and natural history study," Amer. J. Neuroradiol. **15**, 945–950 (1994).
69. B.B. Scott *et al.*, "Vascular dynamics of an experimental cerebral arteriovenous shunt in the primate," Surg. Neurol. **10**, 34–38 (1978).
70. G.J. Hademenos, and T.F. Massoud, "Intranidal hemodynamic compartmentalization of cerebral arteriovenous malformations: Simulations of superselective angiography in a three-dimensional electrical network model," (Manuscript in preparation).
71. J.J. Jafar, A.J. Davis, A. Berenstein, I.S. Choi, and J. Kupersmith, "The effect of embolization with *N*-butyl cyanoacrylate prior to surgical resection of cerebral arteriovenous malformations," J. Neurosurg. **78**, 60–69 (1993).
72. F. Viñuela, J.E. Dion, G. Duckwiler, N.A. Martin, P. Lylyk, A. Fox, D. Pelz, C.G. Drake, J.J. Girvin, and G. Debrun, "Combined endovascular embolization and surgery in the management of cerebral arteriovenous malformations: Experience with 101 cases," J. Neurosurg. **75**, 856–864 (1991).
73. R.F. Spetzler, N.A. Martin, L.P. Carter, R.A. Flom, P.A. Raudzens, and E. Wilkinson, "Surgical management of large AVMs by staged embolization and operative excision,"J. Neurosurg. **67**, 17–28 (1987).

74. R.S. Maurice-Williams, *Subarachnoid Hemorrhage: Aneurysms and Vascular Malformations of the Central Nervous System.* (Wright, Bristol, 1987), p. 307.
75. L.I. Malis, "Arteriovenous malformations of the brain, in *Neurological Surgery*, 2nd ed., edited by J.R. Youmans (Saunders, Baltimore, 1982), Vol. 3, pp. 1786–1806.
76. S. Mullan, F.D. Brown, and N.J. Patronas, "Hyperemic and ischemic problems of surgical treatment of arteriovenous malformations," J. Neurosurg. **51**, 757–764 (1979).
77. A.R. Massaro, W.L. Young, A. Kader, N. Ostapkovich, T.K. Tatemichi, B.M. Stein, and J.P. Mohr, "Characterization of arteriovenous malformation feeding vessels by carbon dioxide reactivity," Amer. J. Neuroradiol. **15**, 55–61 (1994).
78. A.J. Luessenhop, F.M. Ferraz, and L. Rosa, "Estimate of the incidence and importance of circulatory breakthrough in the surgery of cerebral arteriovenous malformations," Neurol. Res. **4**, 177–190 (1982).
79. R.F. Spetzler, C.B. Wilson, P. Weinstein, M. Mehdorn, J. Townsend, and D. Telles, "Normal perfusion pressure breakthrough theory," Clin. Neurosurg. **25**, 651–672 (1978).
80. V.V. Halbach, R.T. Higashida, P. Yang, S. Barnwell, C.B. Wilson, and G.B. Hieshima, "Preoperative balloon occlusion of arteriovenous malformations," Neurosurgery **22**, 301–308 (1988).
81. P.D. Purdy, H.H. Batjer, R.C. Risser, and D. Samson, "Arteriovenous malformations of the brain: Choosing embolic materials to enhance safety and ease of excision," J. Neurosurg. **77**, 217–222 (1992).
82. T.F. Massoud, G.R. Duckwiler, F. Viñuela, and G. Guglielmi, "Acute subdural hemorrhage complicating embolization of a cerebral arteriovenous malformation," Amer. J. Neuroradiol. **15**, 852–856 (1995).
83. R.D. Brown, Jr, D.O. Wiebers, and G.S. Forbes, "Unruptured intracranial aneurysms and arteriovenous malformations: Frequency of intracranial hemorrhage and relationship of lesions," J. Neurosurg. **73**, 859–863 (1990).
84. R. Garcia-Monaco, G. Rodesch, H. Alvarez, Y. Iizuka, F. Hui, P. Lasjaunias, "Pseudoaneurysms within ruptured intracranial arteriovenous malformations: Diagnosis and early endovascular management," Amer. J. Neuroradiol **14**, 315–321 (1993).
85. D. Kondziolka, B.J. Nixon, P. Lasjaunias, W.S. Tucker, K. Terbrugge, and S.M. Spiegel, "Cerebral arteriovenous malformations with associated arterial aneurysms: Hemodynamic and therapeutic considerations," Can. J. Neurol Sci. **15**, 130–134 (1988).
86. G.J. Hademenos, T.F. Massoud, D.J. Valentino, G. Duckwiler, and F. Viñuela, "A non-linear mathematical model for the development and rupture of intracranial saccular aneurysms," Neurol. Res. **16**, 376–384 (1994).
87. L. Leskell, "The stereotaxic method and radiosurgery of the brain," Acta. Chir. (Scand.) **102**, 316–319 (1951).
88. L. Steiner, L. Leskell, T. Greitz, D.M.C. Forster, and E.O. Backlund, "Stereotaxic radiosurgery for cerebral AVMs. Report of a case. Acta Chir. (Scand.) **138**, 459–464 (1972).
89. E.J. Hall, "Factors that modify radiobiological response, in *Stereotactic Radiosurgery Update*, edited by L.D. Lunsford (Elsevier Science, New York, 1992), pp. 11–17.
90. L.D. Lunsford, "Vascular malformations. The role of stereotaxic radiosurgery

in the management of brain vascular malformations, in *Stereotactic Radiosurgery*, edited by E. Alexander III, J.S. Loeffler, and L.D. Lunsford (McGraw-Hill, New York, 1993), pp. 111–121.
91. D.A. Larson *et al.*, "Current radiosurgery practice: Results of an ASTRO survey," Int. J. Radiat. Oncology Biol. Phys. **28**, 523–526 (1994).
92. D. Kondziolka, L.D. Lunsford, E. Kanal, and L. Talagala, "Stereotactic magnetic resonance angiography for targeting in arteriovenous malformation radiosurgery," Neurosurgery **35**, 585–591 (1994).
93. E.J. Hall, and D.J. Brenner, "The radiobiology of radiosurgery: Rationale for different treatment regimes for AVMs and malignancies," Int. J. Radiat. Oncology Biol. Phys. **25**, 381–385 (1993).
94. F. Colombo, F. Pozza, G. Chierego, L. Casentini, G. De Luca, and P. Francescon, "Linear accelerator radiosurgery of cerebral arteriovenous malformations: An update," Neurosurgery **34**, 14–21 (1994).
95. T.F. Massoud, and G.J. Hademenos, "Intranidal hemodynamic perturbations and risk of hemorrhage after radiosurgery of intracranial arteriovenous malformations: A theoretical model. Int. J. Radiat. Oncol. Biol. Phys. (Submitted).
96. M. Yamamoto, M. Jimbo, M. Ide, C. Lindquist, and L. Steiner, "Post-radiation volume changes in gamma unit-treated cerebral arteriovenous malformations," Surg. Neurol. **40**, 485–490 (1993).
97. A. Kader, W.L. Young, J. Pile-Spellman, H. Mast, R.R. Sciacca, J.P. Mohr, and B.M. Stein, the Columbia University AVM Study Project, "The influence of hemodynamic and anatomic factors on hemorrhage from cerebral arteriovenous malformations," Neurosurgery **34**, 801–808 (1994).
98. F. Turjman, T.F. Massoud, F. Viñuela, J.W. Sayre, G. Guglielmi, and G. Duckwiler, "Correlation of the angioarchitectural features of cerebral arteriovenous malformations with clinical presentation of hemorrhage," Neurosurgery **37**, 856–862 (1995).
99. B.E. Pollock, J.C. Flickinger, L.D. Lunsford, D.J. Bissonette, and D. Kondziolka, "Factors that predict the bleeding risk of cerebral arteriovenous malformations," Stroke **27**, 1–6 (1996).
100. R.G. Auger, and D.O. Wiebers, "Management of unruptured intracranial arteriovenous malformations: A decision analysis," Neurosurgery **30**, 561–569 (1992).
101. W.S. Fisher III, "Decision analysis: A tool of the future: An application to unruptured arteriovenous malformations," Neurosurgery **24**, 129–135 (1989).
102. D. Kondziolka, M.R. McLaughlin, and J.R.W. Kestle, "Simple risk predictions for arteriovenous malformation hemorrhage," Neurosurgery **37**, 851–855 (1995).
103. R.C. Wallace, R.A. Flom, M.H. Khayata, B.L. Dean, J. McKenzie, J.C. Rand, N.A. Obuchowski, R.C. Zepp, J.M. Zabramski, and R.F. Spetzler, "The safety and effectiveness of brain arteriovenous malformation embolization using acrylic and particles: The experiences of a single institution," Neurosurgery **37**, 606–618 (1995).
104. R.T. Frizzel, and W.S. Fisher, "Cure, morbidity, and mortality associated with embolization of brain arteriovenous malformations: A review of 1246 patients in 32 series over a 35-year period," Neurosurgery **37**, 1031–1040 (1995).
105. G. Luxton, Z. Petrovich, G. Jozsef, L.A. Nedzi, and M.L.J. Apuzzo, "Stereo-

tactic radiosurgery: Principles and comparison of treatment methods," Neurosurgery **32**, 241–259 (1993).
106. C.S. Ogilvy, "Radiation therapy for arteriovenous malformations: A review," Neurosurgery **26**, 725–735 (1990).
107. S. Nagasawa, M. Kawanishi, H. Tanaka, T. Ohta, S. Nagayasu, and H. Kikuchi, "Haemodynamic study of arteriovenous malformations using a hydraulic model," Neurol. Res. **15**, 409–412 (1993).

7.8 Problems

7.1. The volume of an AVM is sometimes defined clinically as $0.52D_lD_wD_h$, where D is diameter, where l is length, w is width, and h is height. How is 0.52 derived?

7.2. What is a major disadvantage of employing a biomathematical AVM model of a swine to simulate hemodynamics as a result of therapy?

7.3. How is AVM size related to cerebrovascular steal?

7.4. How would the implementation of pulsatile flow change the matrix calculations from electrical network analysis in the simulations of the AVM model described in Sec. 7.4.1.2?

7.5. Why should excision of AFs be performed as close to the nidus boundary as possible?

7.6. Rupture of an arteriovenous fistula is believed to occur toward the venous end. What physical basis would tend to support this clinical observation?

7.7. What would be one way of simulating the effects of tortuosity according to Poiseuille's law?

7.8. Using Poiseuille s law, express the pressure gradient in terms of velocity?

7.9. Given an AVM with two draining veins, such as that represented in the AVM model depicted in Fig. 7.2, occlusion of which DV would be more likely to pose a higher risk of rupture? Explain.

Glossary

Aneurysm A form of cerebrovascular disease that manifests itself as a sac formed by the dilatation or ballooning of the wall of a blood vessel due to structural weakening. If left untreated, the sac continues to expand until it eventually bursts or ruptures, causing hemorrhage.

Angiography Imaging technique in which blood vessels filled with a contrast medium are observed using x-rays. Angiography is used in the diagnostic assessment and the therapeutic endovascular embolization of cerebrovascular diseases such as aneurysms and arteriovenous malformations (AVMs) by permitting the neuroradiologist to visually assess the size and anatomy of the lesion, properly guide and observe the deposition of embolic agent, and monitor the progress and effectiveness of treatment at a particular procedure.

Angioplasty Interventional procedure of remodeling the vascular wall of an atherosclerotic vessel and establishing patency of the vessel lumen.

Anticoagulant A pharmacological agent used in the treatment of some episodes of stroke that retards coagulation or the clotting process of blood. When a blood clot forms and acts as an embolus, stopping flow through the occluded vessel, the anticoagulant is administered to prevent the formation of additional clots or the enlargement of existing clots. It does not, however, act to dissolve the original clot.

Antihypertensive drugs A family of pharmacological agents administered to control high blood pressure or hypertension. Their purpose is to minimize the hemodynamic impact and related forces on the fragile tissue presented by cerebrovascular disease until more permanent therapy or treatment, such as surgery, can be administered.

Aorta The major artery of the circulatory system that transports blood from the left ventricle of the heart to the systemic circulation, feeding all organs and tissues of the human body.

Arterial blood Blood that has been oxygenated in the lungs and transported via the left side of heart to the systemic circulation.

Arterioles The smallest of the artery vessels that lead to capillary beds.

Arteriosclerosis A group of diseases characterized by an accumulation of fibrous tissue, fatty substances (lipids), and/or minerals. These deposits (commonly referred to as atheromata or plaques) form a dense and irregular projection above the inner layer of the artery, and thus decrease the diameter of the internal channel of the vessel, resulting in luminal obstruction of the vessel and loss of elasticity of the vessel wall.

Artery Blood vessels that transport blood away from the heart to the systemic circulation, feeding all organs and tissues of the human body. Arteries usually carry oxygenated blood with the exception of the pulmonary artery, which carries deoxygenated blood from the heart to the lungs for oxygenation.

Arterial feeder An artery that serves as an inlet for blood flow into an arteriovenous malformation (AVM). It is the primary route for embolization treatment of AVMs. Depending on its size and location within the brain, each AVM usually presents with more than one arterial feeder.

Atherectomy Surgical removal of atherosclerotic lesions.

Atheroma Deposit of lipid-containing materials along arterial walls that form the basis for an atherosclerotic lesion.

Autoregulation Inherent biological control exhibited by arteries to regulate blood flow.

AVM Abbreviation for arteriovenous malformation. A form of cerebrovascular disease that consists of a defective or abnormal array of vessels (known collectively as the nidus) connected between an artery and a vein.

Bernoulli's principle Relation describing the conservation of energy of a flowing fluid in a vessel where the total energy (E) present in a flowing fluid is equal to the sum of the pressure energy (P), the gravitational energy (ρgh), and the kinetic energy ($\rho v^2/2$), or stated in equation form is $E = P + \rho v^2/2 + \rho gh$, where ρ is fluid density, v is velocity, g is the gravitational constant, and h is fluid height or depth. In most instances pertaining to physiological applications, the gravitational energy component of Bernoulli's principle is negligible and often omitted. However, Bernoulli's principle is particularly applicable to fluid dynamics within a blood vessel with a sudden contraction or expansion as may be presented by cerebrovascular diseases.

Blood pressure An average measurement of hemodynamic forces exerted against the walls of blood vessels comprising the circulation. Blood pressure is presented typically as two pressures: systolic pressure and diastolic pressure, given as a ratio. The systolic pressure (upper value) is the pressure measured during systole or as the heart contracts. The diastolic pressure is the pressure measured during diastole or as the heart relaxes and refills with circulated blood returning from the large veins. The blood pressure for a normal human is 120 mm Hg/80 mm Hg [(systolic pressure)/(diastolic pressure)].

Capillaries The smallest blood vessels that present as an intricate network or bed of vessels within the tissue and organs to ensure sufficient perfusion, enabling oxygen and nutrients to diffuse into the tissues, and removal of carbon dioxide and waste products from the tissues into the bloodstream.

Cardiac cycle Description of all physiological processes and events that occur during one heartbeat, including contraction, pumping, relaxation, and filling.

Cardiac output A quantitative measure of the volume of blood pumped by the heart out of the left ventricle per minute.

Carotid arteries Major arteries responsible for blood supply to the head, neck, and brain. On each side of the neck are the left and right common carotid arteries, each of which branch into the external carotid artery and the internal carotid artery.

Catheter A long, thin, flexible tube, typically inserted into an artery of the peripheral circulation (arm or leg), that permits access to delicate and fragile regions of the human body, particularly the brain. The catheter is used for the introduction of contrast medium into the circulation for diagnostic and angiographic examination and in the therapeutic treatment of cerebrovascular diseases for the delivery and deposition of embolic agents.

Central venous pressure Vascular pressure exhibited by the central veins.

Cerebrovascular disease Diseases that afflict the blood vessels of the brain.

circle of Willis The pentagonal arrangement of major arteries at the base of the brain that supply blood flow to all cerebral territories.

Coagulation Term describing the physiological processes of blood clot formation.

Collagen A large fibrous protein which, together with elastin, constitutes the dominant structural components for connective tissues throughout the body, including the blood vessels.

Collateral circulation Blood circulation through blood vessels in a region adjacent to or in the vicinity of a stenosed or occluded vessel.

Compliance The ratio of the change of volume to the change in internal pressure experienced by an elastic object.

Compressibility A physical property of fluids pertaining to its change in density while in motion. An incompressible fluid, which is commonly used to characterize blood, exhibits constant density while in motion.

Congenital Term referring to a condition existing at birth, usually before, and is commonly the result of an inherited genetic defect. AVMs are believed to be formed prior to birth and typically become symptomatic in the third or fourth decade of life.

Continuity equation An extension of the conservation of mass which states that the velocity (v) of a flowing fluid of density ρ multiplied by the cross-sectional area A of the vessel or tube is constant at any point along the vessel, or stated in equation form as $\rho_1 A_1 v_1 = \rho_2 A_2 v_2$, where 1 and 2 refer to arbitrary points along the vessel. In most instances, the density of the fluid is assumed constant between points along the vessel and can thus be omitted from the above equation.

Contrast medium A radiopaque substance used in angiography to facilitate the visualization of internal structures. The contrast medium contains usually iodine, which is an element that efficiently absorbs x-rays.

Diastole Stage during the cardiac cycle where the heart relaxes and refills with blood from the venous return.

Dilation (or dilatation) Physical stretching or enlargement of elastic objects (blood vessels) beyond its resting state of equilibrium.

Draining vein A vein that serves as an outlet for blood flow from an arteriovenous malformation. Similar to the observations concerning arterial feeders, it is common for an AVM to have more than one draining vein, but this is dependent on its size and location within the brain.

Elastin A large fibrous protein which, together with collagen, constitutes the dominant structural components for connective tissues throughout the body, including the blood vessels.

Embolic agents Physical, chemical, or mechanical substances introduced into an AVM through an arterial feeder in order to obstruct circulation within the AVM. Examples of embolic agents include polymerizing glue, microparticles, and platinum coils.

Embolism Luminal obstruction of a blood vessel by a clot or other physical substance transported through the bloodstream.

Embolus A physical substance that is the source of a luminal obstruction of a blood vessel. Several examples of emboli include a blood clot, a dislodged atherosclerotic plaque, or an air bubble.

Embolotherapy Therapeutic introduction of a substance (see *Embolic agents*) in order to physically occlude a vessel and stop or restrict blood flow through the vessel.

Endarterectomy Surgical removal of the luminal aspect of a blood vessel, usually containing an atherosclerotic lesion.

Endothelium The thin, cellular lining of the innermost layer of the walls of blood vessels.

Endovascular Term meaning *from within* or *through a blood vessel.* Therapy for the treatment of cerebrovascular diseases is commonly referred to as endovascular embolotherapy in which embolization is performed via catheters introduced through the major vessels in the human body.

Enzymes Complex proteins produced by all living organisms that function as catalysts for specific biochemical processes in the body.

Epidemiology The study of the frequency and distribution of a particular disease in a human population.

Epilepsy A neurological condition caused by irregular electrical activity of the brain that precipitates seizures, loss of consciousness, or other temporary disturbances of the nervous system. Epilepsy may be associated with AVMs.

Etiology The study of the origins and causes of a particular disease process.

Fibrin A protein constituting a major component of a blood clot.

Fibrinogen A protein which, as a substrate, is acted on by specific enzymes in the biochemical reactions responsible for the formation of a blood clot (fibrin).

Fistula An abnormal direct connection between artery and vein causing a rapid shunting of blood. Fistulas can occur as a direct result of vascular trauma in close proximity to an artery and vein and are commonly observed in larger AVMs (> 4 cm in diameter).

Flowmeter An instrument for the experimental measurement of blood flow.

Hemodynamics The study of the movements of blood and of related forces. Hemodynamic parameters that are of critical importance in the study of AVMs include volumetric blood flow rate, flow velocity, transnidal pressure gradient, pressures at the arterial feeders and draining veins, and wall shear stress.

Hemorrhage The uncontrollable escape of blood from a ruptured blood vessel and permeation into the anatomical spaces surrounding the organ and associated structures. Hemorrhage is the most devastating consequence of cerebrovascular lesions, i.e., aneurysms and AVMs, accounting for their high death and disability rates.

Heparin A naturally occurring complex acid that possesses the ability to prevent the clotting of blood. Heparin is an anticoagulant used to prevent the enlargement of an existing clot or the formation of additional clots.

Histopathology The branch of science involved with the minute, microscopic structure, composition, and function of diseased or abnormal tissues.

Hypertension An unstable or persistent elevation of blood pressure above the normal range, i.e., 120 mm Hg/80 mm Hg. The consequences of abnormally high blood pressure include heart strain, arterial damage, and a greater risk of stroke. Commonly referred to as high blood pressure.

Hypotension An unstable or persistent reduction of blood pressure below the normal range, i.e., 120 mm Hg/80 mm Hg. The consequences of abnormally low blood pressure include shock or syncope (fainting). Commonly referred to as low blood pressure.

Impedance A measure of the physical opposition or resistance to periodic or pulsatile flow.

Incidence The extent or frequency of a disease in a given population during a specified period.

Infarct An area of tissue subjected to an insufficient blood supply, resulting in damage or death.

Interventional neuroradiology The branch of radiology in which vessel diseases of the brain are treated endovascularly and usually observed and monitored using angiography.

Intracranial Term referring to a location or space within the cranium or skull.

Intranidal Term referring to a location or space within the nidus of an AVM.

In vitro Latin translation means *in glass*. Term used to describe a phenomenon or experimentation studied in an artificial environment outside a living body under laboratory conditions.

In vivo Latin translation means *in a living body*. Term used to describe a phenomenon or experimentation studied in a living body.

Ischemia A local, usually temporary, reduction of blood supply and corresponding deficiency of oxygen to a region of tissue or organ, often caused by a constriction or a luminal obstruction of a connected blood vessel.

Laminar flow Characteristic laminae or layers exhibited by nonturbulent flow of a viscous fluid.

Lesion Term referring to the entity of diseased or abnormal tissue. An AVM or aneurysm is typically referred to as a cerebrovascular lesion.

Lumen The opening or cross-sectional area of a blood vessel. The term also describes the opening or neck of an aneurysm.

Mass effect Clinical term to describe the effects of a growing, enlarged, and abnormal lesion occupying space within the brain. Depending on the location of the lesion, symptoms may not occur until the brain cannot accommodate additional growth. Mass effect usually manifests itself as neurological symptoms such as headaches, double vision, loss of coordination, etc.

Natural history Summary of all existing knowledge concerning the origin, development, and fate of a disease.

Neurological deficit A debilitating result of a disease directly affecting the nervous system.

Newtonian fluid A fluid that exhibits a constant viscosity at all volumetric flow rates. A non-Newtonian fluid, which accurately characterizes blood, exhibits a changing viscosity in motion.

Nidus A conglomerate of abnormal, enlarged blood vessels situated between an artery and a vein in an arteriovenous malformation (see *AVM*).

Occlusion The act of closure or obstruction of a blood vessel to stop blood flow.

Ohm's law Fundamental law of electricity governing the transfer of current through an elementary resistance. Ohm's law is given in equation form as $V = IR$, where V is the voltage, I is the current, and R is the resistance.

Peripheral resistance Vascular resistance exerted by the vessels in the peripheral circulation to the flow of blood. An increase in peripheral resistance causes a concommitant rise in blood pressure.

Platelets Elements found in blood involved in the formation of blood clots.

Plexiform Resembling a tangled, interwoven network or mesh of interconnected blood vessels.

Poiseuille's law Elementary law of fluid dynamics that describes the constant, laminar volumetric flow rate (Q) of a fluid through a rigid tube in terms of the pressure gradient (ΔP), length (L) and radius (R) of the vessel, and viscosity of fluid (η). Poiseuille's law is given in equation form as $Q = \pi \Delta P R^4 / 8L\eta$, and can often be expressed in its abbreviated form as $\Delta P = QR_v$, where R_v is the vascular resistance.

Pulmonary circulation One of the two types of circulatory pathways, describing the circulation of blood through the lungs. In the pulmonary circulation, blood flows from the right lower chamber of the heart (right ventricle) through the lungs, returning to the left upper chamber of the heart (left atrium).

Pulsatility Term referring to the oscillatory behavior of blood flow continually pumped from the heart in systematic time intervals over a heartbeat.

Pulse pressure Mean blood pressure defined in terms of the systolic and diastolic blood pressures by the following: BP_{mean} = Systolic BP + [2 × (Diastolic BP)]/3.

Radioisotopic scanning A diagnostic technique involving the injection of radioisotopes into the bloodstream and circulation through all tissues and organs. The emitted radioactivity is detected by a scanner and a recorded image of the activity distribution is produced.

Revascularization Removal of luminal obstruction and restoration of sufficient blood flow to body tissues when supplying arteries are narrowed or blocked by injury or disease.

Stasis Cessation or reduction of blood flow through any tissue or organ.

Steal A blood flow or tissue perfusion phenomenon in which an AVM is believed to "steal" blood from the normal circulation of the brain due to the rapid shunting of blood through an AVM.

Stenosis Narrowing or closure of the vascular lumen.

Stroke An impeded or reduced blood supply to some part of the brain, generally caused by (1) blood clot formation within a vessel (thrombosis); (2) a rupture of the blood vessel wall (hemorrhage); or (3) Dislodgement of an atherosclerotic plaque or other substance that flows to the brain and obstructs a vessel (embolism).

Stroke Volume The volume of blood pumped from the heart at each contraction.

Surgical resection Method of treatment for AVMs involving direct entrance into the cranium or skull and precise dissection of the abnormal tissue comprising the AVM to facilitate the redirection of blood flow through the normal brain circulation.

Symptom An indication of abnormal function, sensation, or appearance that provides subjective evidence of the condition of a patient.

Systemic Term pertaining to or affecting the human body as a whole. *Systemic* is used in the context of describing the blood pressure originating from the heart at the onset of a heartbeat.

Systemic circulation One of the two types of circulatory pathways, describing the circulation of blood through all parts of the body. In the systemic circulation, blood flows from the left lower chamber of the heart (left ventricle) through the body, back to the right upper chamber of the heart (right atrium).

Systole Stage during the cardiac cycle where the heart contracts.

Thrombectomy Surgical removal of a blood clot from a blood vessel.

Thrombolytic agents Pharmacological substances that dissolve blood clots.

Thrombosis The formation of a blood clot (thrombus) inside a blood vessel.

Thrombus A blood clot that forms inside a blood vessel.

Tortuosity Term referring to twists and turns in a structure. The vessels within the nidus of a brain AVM are highly tortuous.

Transnidal Term pertaining to measurements across the nidus.

Turbulent flow Motion of a fluid exhibiting randomly fluctuating velocity and pressure.

Vascular resistance An opposing force exerted by the vessel against the flow of fluid through the vessel.

Vein Blood vessel that carries blood from various parts of the body back to the heart. All veins in the body conduct unoxygenated blood except the pulmonary veins, which conduct freshly oxygenated blood from the lungs back to the heart.

Venous blood Blood that is transported through the veins from all parts of the body back to the heart and then pumped by the right side of the heart through the pulmonary artery to the lungs where it is oxygenated.

Ventricle The heart has two of these major pumping chambers: the left ventricle that pumps oxygenated blood through the arteries to the body and the right ventricle that pumps deoxygenated blood through the pulmonary artery to the lungs.

Viscoelasticity An object that exhibits the elastic properties and behavior of both a solid and a fluid.

Viscosity A measurement of the degree of resistance or friction acting in a direction opposite to that of a flowing fluid.

Young's modulus Ratio of longitudinal or tensile stress to tensile strain unique to each elastic object.

Answers to Odd-Numbered Problems

Chapter 1 Mathematics Fundamentals

1.1. (A) Polynomial function. (B) Polynomial function. (C) Exponential function. (D) Trigonometric function. (E) Logarithmic function.

1.3. In terms of rectangular coordinates, the cylindrical coordinates can be written as

$$r = \sqrt{x^2 + y^2}, \quad \phi = \tan^{-1}\left(\frac{y}{x}\right), \quad z = z,$$

while in spherical coordinates, these relations are

$$r = \sqrt{x^2 + y^2 + z^2}, \quad \theta = \cos^{-1}(1/\sqrt{x^2 + y^2 + z^2}), \quad \phi = \tan^{-1}\left(\frac{y}{x}\right).$$

1.5. (A) Distance:

$$\begin{aligned} |\mathbf{x}| &= \sqrt{(A \sin \omega t)^2 + (A \cos \omega t)^2} \\ &= \sqrt{(A^2 \sin^2 \omega t) + (A^2 \cos^2 \omega t)} \\ &= \sqrt{A^2(\sin^2 \omega t + \cos^2 \omega t)} = A \end{aligned}$$

(B) Velocity:

$$\mathbf{v} = \frac{dx}{dt} = \mathbf{i}\, A\omega \cos \omega t - \mathbf{j}\, A\omega \sin \omega t.$$

(C) Speed:

$$v = |\mathbf{v}| = \sqrt{(A^2\omega^2 \cos^2 \omega t + A^2\omega^2 \sin^2 \omega t)} = A\omega.$$

The direction of the angle is defined as

$$\theta = \tan^{-1}\left(\frac{V_y}{V_x}\right),$$

$$\theta = \tan^{-1}\left(\frac{-A\omega \sin \omega t}{A\omega \cos \omega t}\right) = \tan^{-1}\left(-\frac{\sin \omega t}{\cos \omega t}\right).$$

(D) Acceleration:

$$\mathbf{a} = \frac{dy}{dt} = -\mathbf{i}\,A\omega^2 \sin \omega t - \mathbf{j}\,A\omega^2 \cos \omega t.$$

(E) The acceleration is perpendicular to the velocity since the scalar or dot product of the vectors **v** and **a** is 0 or

$$\mathbf{v} \cdot \mathbf{a} = (A\omega \cos \omega t)(-A\omega^2 \sin \omega t) + (-A\omega \sin \omega t)(-A\omega^2 \cos \omega t) = 0.$$

1.7. Implementing the rate of production of the radioactive species into the raidoactive decay equation yields

$$\frac{dN}{dt} = R - \lambda N,$$

$$n = \frac{R}{\lambda}(1 - e^{-\lambda t}).$$

1.9. The projection of $\psi = \mathrm{A}e^{i(\omega t + \phi)}$ along the real axis is $A \cos(\omega t + \phi)$, and $A \sin(\omega t + \phi)$ is the projection along the complex or imaginary axis.

1.11. Since the wave function contains complex values, then the resolved wave function in terms of the complex axis must be used. Figure 1.16 shows the resolved components of a complex vector with the complex component being along the imaginary axis with a value of $\mathrm{i}R \sin \phi$. Thus, the pressure wave function expressed in trigonometric functions is $P = A \sin(2\pi\omega t + \phi)$.

1.13. According to Ohm's law, $V = iR$. Solving for the current i, we have $i = V/R$ or VR^{-1}. Both matrices for i and V are column matrices and can be expressed as

$$[i] = \begin{bmatrix} i_1 \\ i_2 \\ i_3 \end{bmatrix}, \quad [V] = \begin{bmatrix} V_1 \\ V_2 \\ V_3 \end{bmatrix}.$$

We are searching for the solution to i_1, i_2, and i_3 so $[i]$ is fine as written. However, we know what V_1, V_2, and V_3 corresponding to the current components are from the loop equations, and $[V]$ now becomes

$$[V] = \begin{bmatrix} 0 \\ V_1 + V_2 \\ V_2 - V_3 \end{bmatrix}.$$

The order of the matrix for the resistance components is derived from the number of individual current components and the subsequent interactions between each component. From both the nodal and loop equations, the resistance matrix is of order 3 (3×3):

$$[R] = \begin{bmatrix} 1 & -1 & -1 \\ R_1 & R_2 & 0 \\ 0 & R_2 & -R_3 \end{bmatrix}.$$

We now have the properly expressed matrices for the current, voltage, and resistance, and the current can be calculated by solving the system of linear equations in matrix form:

$$[i] = [V][R]^{-1} = \begin{bmatrix} 0 \\ V_1 + V_2 \\ V_2 - V_3 \end{bmatrix} \begin{bmatrix} 1 & -1 & -1 \\ R_1 & R_2 & 0 \\ 0 & R_2 & -R_3 \end{bmatrix}^{-1}.$$

1.15. Multplication of a function by its inverse:

$$\begin{aligned} e^{ix}e^{-ix} &= (\cos x + i \sin x)(\cos x - i \sin x) \\ &= (\cos^2 x + i \sin x \cos x - i \sin x \cos x - i^2 \sin^2 x) \\ &= \cos^2 x - i^2 \sin^2 x = \cos^2 x - (-1)\sin^2 x = \cos^2 x + \sin^2 x = 1. \end{aligned}$$

Chapter 2 The Physics of Elasticity

2.1. The negative sign in the equations make σ positive when the transverse dimensions of the elastic object decrease on longitudinal extension, which is the general case for homogeneous bodies.

2.3. Newton's third law: Forces acting in one direction are compensated or counteracted by forces acting in the opposite direction.

2.5. When subjected to a distending force, the tension exerted by viscous materials is independent of the length distended.

2.7. $E_c(\omega) = |E_c(\omega)|\cos[\phi(\omega)] + i|E_c(\omega)|\sin[\phi(\omega)]$.

Chapter 3 Circulation: Structure and Physiology

3.1. The low pressure protects the alveolar membranes of the lung from damage due to hemodynamic forces.

3.3. In rigid tubes, the pressure reaches high values during systole and falls to zero at diastole. In elastic tubes, the elastic walls absorb part of the stroke volume and act as a buffer against the pressure values experienced during the cardiac cycle, from systole and diastole.

3.5. The resistance of the single tube is given by R_t. The total resistance for the tubes in series is given by

$$R_{t,s} = \frac{R_t}{3} + \frac{R_t}{3} + \frac{R_t}{3} = 3\frac{R_t}{3} = R_t.$$

The total resistance for the tubes in parallel is given by

$$\frac{1}{R_{t,p}} = \frac{1}{\frac{R_t}{3}} + \frac{1}{\frac{R_t}{3}} + \frac{1}{\frac{R_t}{3}} = \frac{3}{\frac{R_t}{3}} = \frac{9}{R_t},$$

$$R_{t,p} = \frac{R_t}{9}.$$

Chapter 4 Hemodynamics: The Physics of Blood Flow

4.1. The radial and polar velocities v_r and v_θ can be calculated from the stream function ψ according to

$$v_r = -\frac{1}{r^2 \sin\theta}\frac{\partial\psi}{\partial\theta} = -\left(-\frac{Ar^4}{r^2 \sin\theta}[2\sin\theta\cos\theta - 2\cos\theta(-\sin\theta)]\right)$$

$$= \frac{Ar^2}{\sin\theta} 2\sin\theta(\cos\theta + \cos\theta) = 4Ar^2\cos\theta,$$

$$v_\theta = \frac{1}{r\sin\theta}\frac{\partial\psi}{\partial r} = -\frac{1}{r\sin\theta}4A^3(\sin^2\theta - \cos^2\theta).$$

4.3. This problem can be solved by starting with Bernoulli's principle,

$$P_1 - P_2 = \frac{\rho v_2^2}{2}\left[1 - \left(\frac{A_2}{A_1}\right)^2\right],$$

and solving for v_2, yielding

$$v_2 = \sqrt{\frac{2(P_1 - P_2)}{\rho\left[1 - \left(\frac{A_2}{A_1}\right)^2\right]}},$$

(B) The viscosity of the fluid.
(C) The volumetric flow rate is the same—constant throughout the entire syringe. This is guaranteed by the continuity equation: fluid entering the throat of the syringe is equal to that exiting the syringe.

4.5. This problem can be solved using the continuity equation $\rho_1 A_1 v_1 = \rho_2 A_2 v_2$, where ρ is the density of blood, A is the cross-sectional area of the vessel, v is velocity, and subscripts 1 and 2 refer to positional locations within the vessel. Since the blood flow is incompressible, $\rho_1 = \rho_2$, and $v_1 = 40\,\text{cm/s}$, $A_2 = A_1/3$ or $A_1/A_2 = 3$. Solving for v_2:

$$v_2 = \frac{A_1 v_1}{A_2} = 3v_1 = 3 \times 40\,\text{cm/s} = 120\,\text{cm/s}.$$

4.7. From $V = Bdv \times 10^{-8}$, where R is the radius of the artery, = 0.25 cm, corresponding to a diameter $d = 2 \times 0.25\,\text{cm} = 0.5\,\text{cm}$; $B = 500\,\text{G}$, and $v = 150\,\text{mm/s} = 15\,\text{cm/s}$, the voltage is

$$V = (0.5\,\text{cm})(500\,\text{G})(15\,\text{cm/s}) \times 10^{-8} = 3750 \times 10^{-8}\,\text{V} = 37.5\,\text{mV}.$$

4.9. Now that the arterial wall is conductive and the generated electric current passes through the wall, the magnetic field becomes markedly reduced in magnitude and the potential difference becomes $V < Bdv \times 10^{-8}$.

4.11. The expression for the voltage from the electromagnetic flowmeter is given as $V = Bdv \times 10^{-8}$. The three criteria are (1) the magnetic field is uniform; (2) the conductor moves in a plane at right angles to the magnetic field; and (3) the length of the conductor extends at right angles to both the magnetic field and direction of motion.

4.13. Yes, because they satisfy Laplace's equation.

4.15. (A) Impedance:

$$Z_n = \frac{P_n(t)}{Q_n(t)} = \frac{P_n e^{i(\omega n t - \phi_n)}}{Q_n e^{i(\omega n t - \theta_n)}} = \frac{P_n}{Q_n} e^{i(\phi_n - \theta_n)}, \quad n = 0, 1, 2, \cdots.$$

(B)

$$\tan\phi = \frac{\text{Im}(Q)}{\text{Re}(Q)}, \quad \tan\theta = \frac{\text{Im}(P)}{\text{Re}(P)}.$$

Chapter 5 The Physics of Stroke

5.1. That the reference line from which distances A and B were determined was not linear—also vessel overlap, improperly acquired images.

5.3. In this case, a normally incident wave implies that $\phi_i = \phi_r = \phi_t = 0$. The ratios are given by

$$\frac{A_r}{A_i} = \frac{Z_2 \cos\phi_i - Z_1 \cos\phi_t}{Z_2 \cos\phi_i + Z_1 \cos\phi_t}, \quad \frac{A_t}{A_i} = \frac{2Z_2 \cos\phi_i}{Z_2 \cos\phi_i + Z_1 \cos\phi_t}.$$

Making the appropriate substitutions, the ratios now become

$$\frac{A_r}{A_i} = \frac{Z_2 - Z_1}{Z_2 + Z_1}, \quad \frac{A_t}{A_i} = \frac{2Z_2}{Z_2 + Z_1}.$$

5.5. On a qualitative basis, the flow rate and pressure gradient across a stenosis are related by Flow rate $\propto \sqrt{\Delta P}$. Consider, now, a twofold increase or doubling of the pressure gradient results in

$$(\% \text{ Increase in flow rate}) \approx (\sqrt{2} - \sqrt{1}) \times 100\%$$
$$\approx (1.4 - 1) \times 100\% \approx 40\%.$$

5.7. The average blood speed is given by $v = Q/\Omega$, where v is the blood flow velocity, Q is the blood flow rate, and Ω is the cross-sectional area of the vessel. Since the flow rate is constant by the continuity equation, $Q_{\text{orig}} = R_{\text{obs}}$, $v_{\text{orig}}\Omega_{\text{orig}} = v_{\text{obs}}\Omega_{\text{obs}}$. In this problem, $v_{\text{orig}} = 100\,\text{cm/s}$, $\Omega_{\text{orig}} = \pi(10\,\text{mm})^2$, and $\Omega_{\text{orig}} = \pi(5\,\text{mm})^2$. Solving for v_{obs},

$$v_{\text{obs}} = v_{\text{orig}} \frac{\Omega_{\text{orig}}}{\Omega_{\text{obs}}} = 100\,\text{cm/s} \times 4 = 400\,\text{cm/s}.$$

Chapter 6 The Physics of Intracranial Aneurysms

6.1. The idea is to find an outlet around the house through which water runs readily such as the kitchen sink, bathtub faucet, or a garden hose. Once the water is turned on and flow through the outlet has been established, slowly place your finger over the outlet to simulate an obstruction. Three things can readily be observed as the finger moves to cover the entire outlet: (1) the amount of water exiting the faucet (volumetric flow rate) is reduced; (2) the speed or velocity of the water is much faster, and (3) the velocity distribution of water becomes much more diffuse, spread out, and erratic.

6.3. The primary objective in embolization is to fully occlude the aneurysm so that flow will be redirected through the parent vessel without further causing damage to the aneurysm wall. A partially embolized aneurysm creates an unusual geometry within the vasculature promoting abnormal hemodynamics and the high probability of a residual or daughter aneurysm occurring from the primary aneurysm.

6.5. The hypothetical drug would most likely act to halt the biochemical degradation of the structural proteins collagen and elastin in the aneurysm wall by inhibiting the activity of collagenase and elastase. The drug could also promote the biochemical growth of collagen or elastin.

6.7. Abdominal aortic aneurysms develop along the aorta which is the largest vessel in the human body and is connected directly to the heart. In comparison to an intracranial aneurysm, rupture of an AAA pumps a larger volume of blood into the abdominal cavity at a much more rapid rate. A corresponding rapid drop in blood pressure occurs, inducing hypovolemic shock, cardiac arrest, and ultimately death. Although surgical treatment does exist for ruptured AAAs, it must be implemented immediately following rupture for any kind of successful patient outcome.

6.9. Laplace's law for an elastic sphere exhibiting $h \approx R$ would be

$$S = (P_i R_i/2h) - (P_O R_O/2h) = (P_i R_i - P_O R_O)/2h$$

where the subscripts i and o correpsond to values at the inner and outer regions of the aneurysm wall, respectively.

6.11. Laplace's law defines a relationship between the circumferential stress of the aneurysm wall and the radius and is given, for a spherical elastic object, as:

$$S = PR/2h \qquad (1)$$

where S is the stress, P is the pressure, R is the aneurysm radius, and h is the wall thickness. Stress is also described in terms of the strain, ε, defined by:

$$S = E\varepsilon = E(R/R_i) = (R - R_i)/R_i \qquad (2)$$

where R is the final or current radius and R_i is the initial radius. Using Eqs. (1) and (2), the stress and strain of an elastic structure are used to describe the elastic modulus, E:

$$E = \text{stress/strain} = [PR/2t]/[(R - R_i)/R_i] = [PRR_i]/[2tR - 2tR_i] \qquad (3)$$

6.13. The higher the elastic modulus implies a stronger and stiffer aneurysm wall and a much higher resonant frequency, as is shown from Eq. (6.47).

6.15. The effects of thrombosis on the hemodynamics within an aneurysm include the following: (1) to act as a "shock absorber", protecting the structurally fatigued aneurysm wall from further damage; and (2) to redirect blood flow along the parent vessel.

6.17. The magnetic field created by a current loop of radius R at points a distance x along its axis is given by (Halliday D, Resnick R. *Fundamentals of Physics,*

Second Edition. New York: John Wiley & Sons; 1981: pp. 566–567):

$$B(x) = (\mu_0/2)[iR^2/(R^2 + x^2)^{3/2}]$$

where μ_0 is the permeability constant ($= 4\pi \times 10^{-7}$ T m/A).

6.19. Water is collected in an appropriate container for a predefined time, e.g., 1 minute. The volume of collected water is divided by the collection time yielding cm^3/min or ml/min.

6.21. Transverse waves.

6.23. For a fusiform aneurysm, we are faced with, in essence, two different volumes. The first volume, V_{AN}, is the volume of the aneurysm approximated as the volume of an ellipsoid:

$$V_{AN} = (4/3)\pi R^3 = (4/3)\pi \text{ Size} * \text{Length}$$

The second volume, V_{LU}, is the volume of the embedded lumen again approximated as the volume of an ellipsoid:

$$V_{LU} = (4/3)\pi\, TL^2 * \text{Length}$$

where TL is the true lumen. The volume of the thrombus, V_{TH}, can be estimated by subtracting V_{LU} from V_{AN} or

$$V_{TH} = V_{AN} - V_{LU} = \{(4/3)\pi \text{ Size} * \text{Length}\} - \{(4/3)\pi\, TL^2 * \text{Length}\}$$

$$= (4/3)\pi * \text{Length}\{\text{Size} - TL^2\}$$

Chapter 7 The Physics of Intracranial Arteriovenous Malformations

7.1. This problem involves the substitution of diameter for radius into the expression for the AVM volume:

$$\text{Volume of AVM} = \frac{4}{3}\pi R_l R_w R_h = \frac{4}{3}\pi \frac{D_1}{2}\frac{D_w}{2}\frac{D_h}{2}$$

$$= \frac{4}{3}\pi\frac{1}{8} D_l D_w D_h = 0.52 D_1 D_w D_h.$$

7.3. According to the mathematical equation presented in Sec. 7.3.2.1,

$$F_b = F_{\text{tot}} - F_{\text{AVM}} = F_{\text{tot}} - \text{CPP}/R_{\text{avm}},$$

a large AVM exhibits a large resistance that decreases the flow through the AVM and increases the flow through the adjacent brain regions. Thus, smaller AVMs are more likely to demonstate cerebrovascular steal.

7.5. The farther away from the nidus along the AF increases the likelihood that branches supplying functional brain may exist.

7.7. Increasing the vessel length by a tortuosity constant.

7.9. In the biomathematical model presented in Fig. 7.2, one DV is drained by the intranidal fistula (DV1) while the other DV, DV2, is drained by plexiform vessels. The intranidal fistula is an enlarged vessel and assumes the majority of the hemodynamic load through the AVM. Occlusion of DV1 causes a redistribution of blood to the smaller, plexiform vessels that must now accommodate the added hemodynamic burden in addition to their usual load. The plexiform vessels cannot readily handle the redistribution of blood from a structural standpoint and are thus more likely to rupture than occlusion of the DV2. As DV2 is occluded, the redistribution of blood causes a minor contribution to blood exiting DV1 via the intranidal fistula, and thus biomechanical stress of the affected nidus vessels increases only slightly, if any, and the vessels are less likely to rupture.

Subject Index